Grandma's Country Scrapbook

DEDICATION

This book is dedicated to my grandmother for her fruit cake, my aunt
for her parsley scones, my mother-in-law for her sponge cake and
my mother for her meringues.

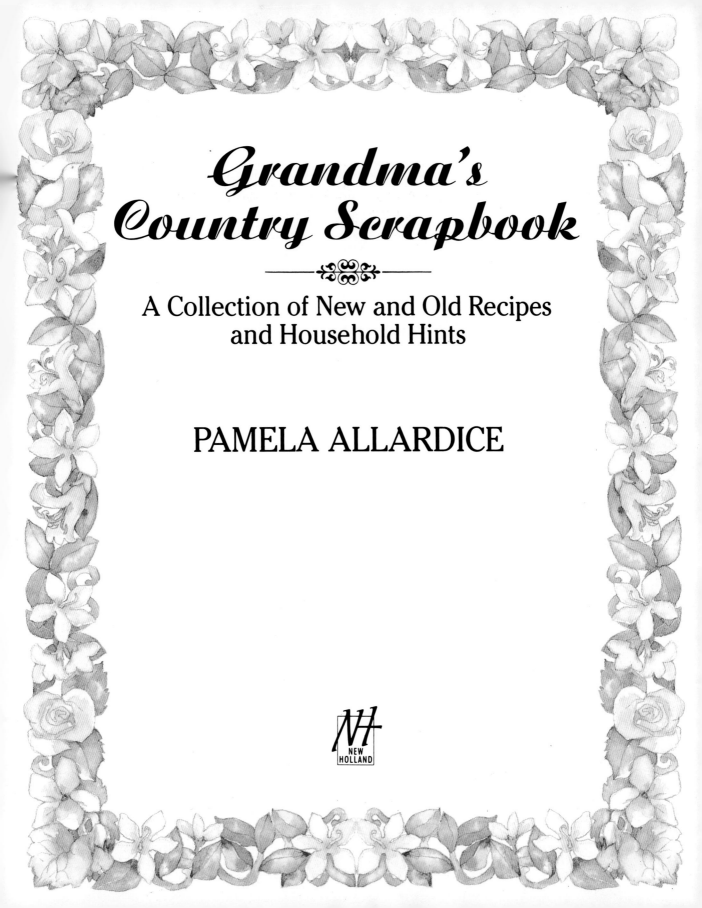

Grandma's Country Scrapbook

A Collection of New and Old Recipes and Household Hints

PAMELA ALLARDICE

NH
NEW
HOLLAND

SPECIAL NOTE

While all care has been taken to ensure the accuracy of the information presented here, the author and publisher accept no responsibility for the effectiveness or otherwise of any of the remedies herein. All plants and foods, like all medicines, may be dangerous if used improperly. The simple traditional remedies in this book must not be used as substitutes for professional medical attention to any serious health disturbance. When in doubt, consult your doctor.

Homemade beauty products like the ones described in this book contain no artificial preservatives, so to make them last as long as possible, always store in sterilised, airtight jars. Keep only for one or two days in the refrigerator and be sure to use the freshest ingredients.

Similarly, cookery ingredients, such as flour and certain fruits, vary depending on brand and season. The measurements for ingredients in the recipes given here are in many instances expressed in a traditional fashion and are a guide only — the choice is yours to adjust sweetness, tartness, thickness and so on.

First published in the UK in 1992 by
New Holland (Publishers) Ltd
37 Connaught Street, London W2 2AZ

First published in 1992 by Simon & Schuster Australia
20 Barcoo Street, East Roseville NSW 2069

Copyright © 1992 Pamela Allardice
Copyright © 1992 in Illustrations Helen McCosker

ISBN 1 85368 214 4

Designer: Michelle Havenstein
Illustrator: Helen McCosker
Phototypeset by The Type Group Pty Ltd
Printed and bound in Singapore by Times Offset

Contents

Introduction

Piccalilli, rose petal jam and tasty pumpkin pie . . . spice bouquets, cottage loaves, fragrant bath bags and sleepy-pillows . . . wildflower jellies, old-fashioned sweets, herb vinegars and butters and sweetly scented potpourri . . .

Recipes and household hints passed from one generation to another are often the best you can get. This is especially the case if Grandma was country-bred, for, as country folk are quick to claim, their pickles are the spiciest, their sponge cakes the lightest and their puddings the plummiest!

Grandma was usually a keen and loving gardener, who knew that flowers and herbs could be put to numerous uses about the house. The simplest food can be greatly enhanced by the flavours of a few carefully chosen herbs. Leaves and flowers can be pressed and used to decorate candles, greeting cards and placemats. Scented blossoms add fragrance to pretty pillows, while herbs and flowers combine in effective beauty products just like Grandma used to make.

This book is a collection of traditional crafts that have been translated into modern pursuits. Bringing together excerpts from old herbals and cookery books and wonderful notions for using herbs, spices, flowers and fruit around the home, it has been compiled to share the recipes, craft ideas and folklore of a bygone era.

1
Around the Home

Freshening the Home

The simplest way to perfume the home is with pots or vases of sweet-scented flowers. Gather delicate pink roses, lavender and some crinkly green mint for a tiny vase on the dressing table; hang bunches of aromatic herbs such as rosemary and woodruff in the kitchen to keep the air fresh and to deter flies. Twist fresh herbs and daisies into plaited bands and use as napkin rings, or drop miniature bouquets of lemon verbena, mint, lemon-scented gum and scented pelargonium leaves into finger bowls for the dinner table.

Decorative Wreath.

The canes pruned from grape vines can be woven together easily to form the base for a wreath, and they look so attractive they need little decoration. If you do not have grape vines, try wistaria, willow or birch stems. If you do not have these in your garden either, crumple fine wire mesh into a roll and press into a circular shape. Alternatively, buy a stout wire-and-oasis ring from a craft shop.

Decorate your wreath by tucking in tiny bundles of herbs, flowers and grasses. By starting at one side and working around, all the herbs will travel in the same direction, overlapping to conceal the stems. Rosemary and sage turn a most attractive silvery-grey and banksias dry to a soft pale fawn — all three work well as a background. Add colour to the wreath with flowering herbs such as lavender or clove pinks, or bright plants such as everlasting daisies or marigolds. The delicate oval seeds of Sweet Honesty and the lacily edged crisp pods of Love-in-the-Mist provide a dainty contrast, too.

Stitch or tie a loop of satin ribbon to the top of the wreath with which to hang it.

Spice Wreath

A spice wreath is a colourful and decorative kitchen feature, giving a country air even if you live in the city. A boon for the keen cook, it provides easy access to dried herbs and spices.

Prepare base as for Decorative Wreath, and pad with florist's moss or raffia to disguise the base, then select from the following dried herbs, fruits and spices:

vanilla pods
bunches of cinnamon bark
nutmeg
whole allspice
star anise
fennel
bay leaves
ginger
poppy seed cases
unshelled nuts, eg, almonds

tiny bags homemade
bouquet garni
garlic cloves
lavender flowers
rosemary sprigs
dried chillies
everlasting flowers, eg:
chamomile daisies, gypsophila
small pine cones

Secure the bundles of dried herbs and spices attractively around the wreath by wiring or tying onto the frame with raffia, where necessary. Fresh herbs can also be introduced to the spice wreath by attaching two or three tiny terracotta pots to the frame and planting little clumps of sage or thyme in them. For the really talented craftsperson, use leftover spices and leaves to create imaginative "flowers" — with "petals" of bay leaves surrounding a central "bud" of a walnut, for instance. Spray with gold paint and attach the flowers with gold braid to make the wreath look really festive and glittering for a Christmas gift.

Fresh Eucalypt Potpourri

A light summery mixture which is also fresh and sweet in any sick room where the patient has a cold in the head. The dried flowers are very pretty too. You may like to freshen the mixture with a few drops of lavender oil if you feel its scent is not as strong as you'd like it to be.

100 g/3½ oz dried lavender
* flowers*
50 g/1¾ oz lemon-scented
* tea-tree leaves*
50 g/1¾ oz crumbled
* eucalyptus leaves*
50 g/1¾ oz dried eucalyptus
* flowers*

50 g/1¾ oz lemon thyme
2 tbsp crushed lemon peel
1 tsp ground cloves
1 tsp ground allspice
2 tbsp orris root powder

Scented Pincushion

Slip a scented herb sachet made from muslin or lawn into your pincushion, and every time you press a pin or needle home, a puff of scent will be released, perfuming both the work and you.

30 g/1 oz rosemary
30 g/1 oz hyssop
15 g/½ oz lavender flowers
15 g/½ oz marjoram

1 tsp each crushed cloves and
* ground nutmeg*
1 tbsp orris root powder

A COMFORTABLE POMANDER FOR THE BRAINE — Take Labdanum one ounce, Benjamin and Storax of each two ounces, Damaske powder finely searced one Dram, Cloves and Mace of each a little, a Nutmeg and a little Camphire, Muske and Civet a little. First heate your Morter and pestle with coales, then make them verie cleane and put in your labdanum, beate it well till it waxe softe, put to it two or three drops of oyl of spike and so labour them a while: then put in all the rest finely in powder, and worke them till all be incorporated, then take it out, anoynting your hands with Civet, roll it up and with a Bodkin pierce a hole thorow it.

From *Ram's Little Dodoen* (1606)

Orange and Clove Pomander

The word "pomander" is derived from the French *pomade,* meaning "apple shaped". It is attributed to Henry V who was never seen without a "ball of gold" packed with musk grains and spices he acquired after his victory at Agincourt. Like potpourri, pomanders have a long history of use as ornaments, to cure insomnia, and as antiseptic agents. Hang these pretty, sweet-smelling fruits in your linen press, place a selection of them in a wicker basket near a window, or fold them amongst handkerchiefs in your drawers. Cumquats make delightful miniature pomanders for a change, as do limes, underripe mandarins and small grapefruit.

30 g/1 oz cloves
1 large orange
orris root powder

cinnamon powder
1.5 cm/⅝ in ribbon

Use a toothpick or skewer to make holes for the cloves all over the skin of the fruit. Insert cloves, leaving a cross-shaped space where the ribbon will be bound around the fruit. Dust the orange with equal quantities of orris root powder and cinnamon powder, wrap in tissue and leave to dry for 3–6 weeks. For decoration, glue dried flowers, berries and a cinnamon stick to a satin ribbon tied to the top of the pomander.

Tussie-Mussies

In earlier times, a tussie-mussie, or bouquet of herbs and flowers, was carried in an attempt to repel disease and to overcome the stench of less than wholesome streets and homes. By the Victorian era, pretty posies of flowers were often exchanged as lovers' troth-tokens. Queen Victoria's own wedding bouquet contained sprigs of myrtle, the symbol of love, and heather, for fidelity.

Traditionally, tussie-mussies are posies that are arranged in several concentric circles of colour around a large central flower, such as a rose or a group of tiny flowers, and edged with soft foliage, such as maidenhair fern. Turn the posy slowly as you arrange the flowers, so each ring of blooms overlaps slightly. To finish, tie firmly with pastel satin ribbon.

Perfumed Pyjama Case

When Grandma made a case for storing her night attire, she would fill the space between the lining and the outer case with a blend of sweet-scented petals and herbs. This perfumes the sheets and enfolds the bed in a delicate cloud of fragrance all night long. When making your own scented case, choose pretty cotton or silk to match your bed linen, and edge the case with ribbon and lace.

30 g/1 oz lavender flowers
30 g/1 oz thyme
30 g/1 oz rose petals
1 tbsp clove pink petals

15 g/½ oz dried lemon verbena
leaves
1 tsp ground cloves
1 tbsp orris root powder

Flowers may be kept very fresh over night if they are excluded from the air. To do this, wet them thoroughly, put in a damp box, and cover with wet, raw cotton or wet newspaper, then place in a cool spot.

From *The Dawn* by Louisa Lawson "Household Hints" (c. 1888–1895)

Scented Coathangers

In Grandma's day, lavender was used to protect precious linen and clothing from potentially destructive insects, such as moths. This is why, even today, lavender is the herb most often used for hanging with clothes. Fill a muslin bag the length of your coathanger with lavender or a lavender sachet mix like this one:

1 tbsp lavender flowers	*dried crushed peel of 1 orange*
1 tbsp sweet marjoram	*1 tsp ground nutmeg*
1 tsp each thyme and bergamot	*1 tbsp orris root powder*
1 crumbled bay leaf	

Sew muslin bag in place on the side of the hanger. Wrap wadding around the bag and hanger before covering with pretty silk, organza or muslin. For a finishing touch swing a tiny "swete bag" of lace-trimmed matching fabric embroidered with your initials or those of the recipient — from the hook.

> *Have friends not for the sake of receiving, but of giving*

&❧ Place a drop of scented flower oil on a light bulb. When it is switched on and becomes warm, the scent will fill the whole room.

&❧ Make a roaring log fire in the evening a "scentual" experience by tossing a handful of potpourri on the flames to freshen the room. A charming house-warming gift is bunches of dried rosemary, lemon balm and thyme, bundled together and labelled for this purpose.

&❧ Flies will avoid your house if it is filled with the wholesome scent of peppermint. Add a few drops to a jug of water and place it in the corner of a room. Woodruff also helps keep flies away. John Gerard wrote that bunches of aromatic woodruff ". . . hanged up in houses, doth very well attemper the aire. . ."

🍃 Arrange dried aromatic flowers and leaves in pretty containers — keep an eye out for wicker baskets, old copper kettles, earthenware crocks or pewter mugs. Or hang bunches from the rafters, or by your mantelpiece where the warmth of a fire will enhance the fragrance. Sprinkle a few drops of your favourite scented oil on the arrangement if the aroma starts to fade.

🍃 The Victorians dearly loved perfuming rooms with sweet-scented herbs and flowers and, being sentimentalists, woven garlands of lavender, rosemary and evergreen boughs were hung about the portrait of the family founder on important occasions, such as Christmas, Easter, birthday or family celebrations.

Flower-filled Pillows

The Romans were the first to add dried rose petals to pillows, while Elizabethan mattresses were usually padded with Lady's Bedstraw *(Galium verum)*. His Majesty George III was said to rely upon a hop-scented pillow to ". . . relieve him from that protracted wakefulness under which he laboured for so long a time". Victorian ladies delighted in lavender cushions, turning their faces toward the sweet scent to avert an attack of "the vapours".

Fragrant, flower-filled pillows delicately perfume the bedroom, calm jangled nerves and soothe fractious babies. Prettily scented sachets also have a place in every home. Hang them wherever they may be occasionally brushed against or where passersby will be tempted to squeeze them to release their scent. Use a variety of fabrics to make your "swete bagges", sachets, sleep pillows and such. Gingham, sprigged muslin and fine floral lawn are all suitable, and may be decorated with old-fashioned cross-stitch designs or embroidered initials. Experiment with shapes and sizes, too. How about a lacy, heart-shaped pillow filled with heady jasmine and rosebuds for Saint Valentine's Day? Or a soft bolster filled with a calming, sleep-inducing mixture of woodruff, chamomile and rosemary for a new mother to lean against while nursing her baby? The possibilities are only limited by your imagination . . .

Do not put herb and flower mixtures directly into the decorative cushion cover. Instead, make a case of closely woven material that is sewn up on three sides, with a gap on the fourth side to turn it inside out. After doing this, put the mixture into the case and sew up the open seam before placing inside decorative case. With all the recipes provided here, crush herbs and flowers together in a bowl, mixing thoroughly but gently, then mix in 2–3 drops of essential oil and the orris root powder required. You might also like to add a few drops of brandy to strengthen the scent.

Country Pillow

A warm, relaxing scent — try this in the guest's bedroom or as a "welcome" in a pretty dish by the front door.

30 g/1 oz woodruff
15 g/½ oz hops
15 g/ ½ oz southernwood
6 eucalyptus leaves, crumbled
2 tbsp ground cinnamon

2 tsp cloves
1 tbsp orris root powder
essential oils — vetiver,
*   honeysuckle*

To Make A Sweet Bag For Linen — Take of Orris Roots, Sweet Calamus, cypress roots, of dried lemon-peel, and dried orange-peel; of each a pound; a peck of dried roses; make all these into a grosse powder; coriander seed four ounces, nutmegs an ounce and a half, an ounce of cloves; make all these into fine powder and mix with the other; add musk and ambergris; then take four large handfuls of lavender flowers dried and rubbed; of sweet marjoram, orange-leaves, and young walnut leaves of each a handful, all dried and rubb'd: mix all together, with some bits of cotton perfum'd with essences and put it up into silk bags to lay with your Linnen.

From *The Compleat Housewife* by E. Smith (1736)

Spice Pillow

A tangy, refreshing and slightly sharp mixture. Use in the living room or hall.

30 g/1 oz lavender *2 tsp allspice berries, crushed*
30 g/1 oz rose petals *½ tsp nutmeg, grated*
15 g/½ oz rose geranium leaves *1 tbsp crushed cinnamon*
15 g/½ oz spearmint leaves *1 tbsp orris root powder*
1 tsp crushed cloves *essential oil — lavender*

Quiet Sleep Pillow

A gentle and relaxing mix to calm and lull whirling thoughts.

30 g/1 oz rosemary flowers *2 tsp cloves, crushed*
30 g/1 oz jasmine *1 tsp aniseed*
30 g/1 oz lavender flowers *1 tbsp orris root powder*
15 g/½ oz chamomile flowers *essential oil — bergamot*
1 tbsp marjoram

Headache Pillow

This is cleansing and refreshing for a patient feeling poorly with a cold or the flu.

50 g/1¾ oz dried violets *15 g/½ oz spearmint leaves*
15 g/½ oz dried lime flowers *1 tbsp orris root powder*
15 g/½ oz bergamot *essential oils — carnation and*
15 g/½ oz lemon verbena *violet*

17

Travel Pillow

Very effective in calming the fears or car sickness of poor travellers.

50 g/1¾ oz lavender flowers
50 g/1¾ oz southernwood
50 g/1¾ oz peppermint
30 g/1 oz lemon verbena
30 g/1 oz meadowsweet
15 g/½ oz rosemary
1–2 tbsp crushed lemon peel

1 tbsp crushed cardamom
1 tbsp marjoram
1 tbsp cloves, crushed
1–2 tbsp orris root powder
essential oils — peppermint or
    lemon verbena

Nursery Pillow

50 g/1¾ oz pink rose petals
50 g/1¾ oz sweet woodruff
30 g/1 oz lavender flowers
30 g/1 oz rose-scented geranium
    leaves
15 g/½ oz orange blossom
15 g/½ oz lemon balm
2 tbsp crushed cinnamon

1 tbsp crushed orange peel
1 tbsp crushed lemon peel
1 tbsp allspice berries, crushed
1 tbsp cloves, crushed
2 tbsp orris root powder
essential oils — rose and orange
    blossom

Lovers' Pillow

A warm, dusky, sweet blend, reported to have aphrodisiac properties...

250 g/9 oz peony petals
125 g/4½ oz rose buds
125 g/4½ oz jasmine flowers
30 g/1 oz orange flowers
30 g/1 oz chamomile flowers

30 g/1 oz linden flowers
1 tsp sandalwood
1 tsp allspice
1 tbsp orris root powder
essential oils — rose and
    patchouli

A BAG TO SMELL UNTO FOR MELANCHOLY, OR TO CAUSE ONE TO SLEEP — Take drie Rose leaves, keep them close in a glasse which will keep them sweet, then take powder of Mints, powder of Cloves in a grosse powder, and put the same to the Rose leaves, then put all these together in a bag, and take that to bed with you and it will cause you to sleep, and it is good to smell unto at other times.

From *Ram's Little Dodoen* (1606)

A Pillow for the Sinusitis Sufferer

*50 g/1¾ oz crushed pine
    needles*
30 g/1 oz lemon thyme
30 g/1 oz peppermint
30 g/1 oz rosemary
15 g/½ oz lemon verbena
2 tbsp crushed lemon peel

*1 tbsp crushed eucalyptus
    leaves*
2 tsp nutmeg chips
1 tbsp orris root powder
*essential oils — eucalyptus,
    peppermint or tea tree*

Deckchair Pillow

A fresh green mixture from the herb garden. Use when sitting out of doors as it will help keep insects away.

30 g/1 oz lavender flowers
30 g/1 oz lemon verbena
50 g/1¾ oz lemon thyme
50 g/1¾ oz lemon balm
25 g/1 oz rosemary
15 g/½ oz wormwood
15 g/½ oz peppermint

*1 tbsp cardamom seeds,
    crushed*
dash cinnamon
1–2 bay leaves, crushed
2 tbsp orris root powder
*essential oils — lemon and
    lavender*

My Favourite Mixture

Very soft and sweet for the living room or nursery.

50 g/1¾ oz dried magnolia flowers   1 vanilla pod, crushed
50 g/1¾ oz pink rose petals   1 tsp cloves
50 g/1¾ oz peony flowers   2 tbsp orris root powder
30 g/1 oz carnation flowers   essential oils — carnation and
15 g/½ oz dried lily of the valley   lily of the valley

Cat's Cushion

Wormwood keeps away fleas and most cats find catnip thoroughly irresistible. In 1636, herbalist John Gerard noticed that ". . .cats are very much delighted herewith, for the smell of it is so pleasant unto them, that they rub themselves upon it, and wallow or tumble in it, and also feed on the branches and leaves very greatly. . ."

50 g/1¾ oz catmint   1 tbsp mint
15 g/½ oz wormwood   1 tbsp southernwood
15 g/½ oz lemon verbena   essential oil — lemon verbena

If the family pet is a dog, substitute dried rue for the catmint and increase the amount of southernwood to 50 g/1¾ oz — this mixture will help reduce "doggy smells" in the animal's basket.

Oriental Rose Pillow

A rich, sweet and slightly exotic mixture for the bedroom or study.

50 g/1¾ pink rose petals
30 g/1 oz rose-scented geranium
*   leaves*
30 g/1 oz jasmine flowers
30 g/1 oz hibiscus flowers
30 g/1 oz orange blossom
30 g/1 oz sweet basil
1 tbsp sandalwood raspings

1 tbsp coriander seeds, crushed
1 tsp powdered ginger
1 tsp aniseed
1 cinnamon stick, crumbled
1–2 tbsp orris root powder
essential oils — jasmine and
*   ylang-ylang*

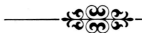

Scented Signatures

Scented paper should not only be just for lining the shelves of the linen press. It is easy to perfume wrapping paper, even tissues, by storing them with bags of dry potpourri mixture. Scented notepaper may be kept for your own use and also makes a pretty present. Buy a box of flower-decorated notelets, open it and insert a couple of small, flat sachets of dry potpourri between the sheets. Seal the box with plastic wrap and leave for three months before using. If the notepaper is intended as a gift, wrap the box in paper perfumed with the same scent, colour-matched if you wish — mauve for the smell of violets, yellow for jasmine, and so on.

Lemon Verbena Ink

1 handful dried lemon verbena   *1 small bottle dark green ink*

Stir lemon verbena through ink in a small, stainless steel saucepan. Simmer for 1 hour, adding 2–3 tablespoonfuls of water. Strain, pressing flowers down well in sieve. Pour scented ink back into bottle.

Lavender and Hyssop Ink

Make as for Lemon Verbena Ink, but substitute 15 g/½ oz each of lavender flowers and hyssop.

Jasmine Notepaper and Ink

Store sheets of paper and envelopes, preferably tinted soft gold, in a box, liberally sprinkling each layer with jasmine flowers. An olde-worlde crinkled effect may be given to the paper by misting with a spray of jasmine perfume before drying.

Decorate notepaper by mounting a few dried jasmine flowers onto each sheet with transparent craft glue. A charming accessory is jasmine-scented ink — add 1 teaspoon jasmine essence to a bottle of coloured ink for truly purple prose!

Greeting Cards and Gift Tags

These can be made from flower-scented paper or light card and cut to any shape — for example, square, oval, circular — which suits the design you have in mind. Cut out with pinking shears and add a pretty ribbon loop in a complementary colour. Add a final personal touch by decorating the tag or card with dried or pressed flowers, or use dried leaves and petals themselves as the labels or tags. Large maple or gum leaves and fully blown rose petals may be pressed until the sap has gone and they are crisp like paper. Write your message using dark grey or green scented ink, pressing carefully so the leaf or petal is not cracked.

A gift by friendship's hand proffered is
to the costliest jewel preferred

Rosemary Bookmarks

As the old saying goes:

> Rosemary is for remembrance
> Between us day and night
> Wishing I may always
> Have you in my sight

As a bonus for the book lover, rosemary's strong scent helps keep moths and silverfish at bay, too.

Mount sprigs of dried rosemary on a backing of stiff parchment or coarse linen. Dried cornflowers and delphiniums both keep their colour well and look attractive with the grey-green rosemary. Cover bookmark with clear self-adhesive plastic, finishing the edges with bias binding, lace or grosgrain ribbon. Glue or tie a length of toning ribbon or silk cord at the top.

Colours of Nature

Although the origins of the art of fabric dyeing are unknown, it was an established craft in China by 3000 BC, while madder and indigo were recorded as being used in India and Egypt in 2500 BC. Since then, chemical dyes have produced longer lasting colours, but they never seem to quite match the depth and lustre of colours derived from the leaves, petals and roots of various herbs and flowers.

Most plants yield some colour as a dye and have an affinity for natural fibres. Wool and silk are best, as they take colours more evenly than the tough, tightly woven fibres of cotton. Parsley and turmeric produce various shades of yellow, for instance, as do agrimony and comfrey; tansy and sorrel give a greener hue; pinks and purples come from madder blended with hollyhock flowers. The fermented foliage of woad gives a beautifully soft blue-grey. Many vegetables, such as onions and red cabbage, may also be used for dyes. Herbs which are not commonly grown in the garden can usually be bought dried from a herbalist or a good craft supplier.

A mordant, or fixative, is always necessary to tap nature's dyepot to its full potential. The principal mordants are alum, tin and iron — alum is probably the easiest to prepare for initial experimentation.

Golden Wool Bath

Prepare a dye bath by placing 100 g/3½ oz dried marigold petals or 300 g/10½ oz fresh flower heads in a muslin bag. Put in a 5-L/1 gall capacity enamel bucket and cover with water (ideally rain or spring water, as chemicals present in water mains can interfere with the process). Let stand overnight.

The next day, fill the bucket to the rim with water and bring slowly to the boil over 1 hour. Simmer for a further hour, cool and strain.

Dissolve 30 g/1 oz alum and 5 g/⅙ oz cream of tartar in warm water and pour mixture through 100 g/3½ oz of raw wool yarn which has been thoroughly wetted and tied loosely into a hank. Simmer for 45 minutes. Drain wool and leave wrapped in plain cloth for a day or two. Rinse thoroughly and then soak yarn in dye mixture, ensuring it is completely submerged. Increase heat and simmer.

When wool has reached desired depth of colour, remove and gently squeeze, don't wring, out excess dye. Rinse wool in another bucket of warm water, and then one of cold — not under a running tap. Hang up to dry in a warm shady place, well away from direct heat or sunlight.

Plants for Dyeing

A garden filled with dye plants is a pretty sight, as many of them are richly coloured. Here is a list of possibilities:

PLANT	PART USED	COLOUR DERIVED FROM DIFFERENT MORDANTS
Agrimony *Agrimonia eupatoria*	tops	fawn with chrome; brown/grey with iron
Bloodroot *Sanguinaria canadensis*	root	red with alum; orange with tin
Comfrey *Symphytum officinale*	leaves	yellow with tin
Dandelion *Taraxacum officinale*	roots and leaves	yellow with tin; grey with iron

PLANT	PART USED	COLOUR DERIVED FROM DIFFERENT MORDANTS
Dyer's Chamomile *Anthemis tinctoria*	flowers	yellow with alum; orange with chrome
Elderberry *Sambucus nigra*	fruit	deep blue or purple with alum
Juniper *Juniperus communis*	berries	cream or beige with alum
Lady's Bedstraw *Galium verum*	roots	rusty colour with alum
Madder *Rubia tinctorum*	roots	bright red with alum; plum with chrome
Marigold *Calendula officinalis*	flowers	yellow with alum; warm beige with chrome
Meadowsweet *Filipendula ulmaria*	roots	black with alum
Onion *Allium cepa*	skins	yellow with alum; dark brown with iron
Parsley *Petroselinum crispum*	tops	gold/green with alum; pale green with chrome
Sorrel *Rumex acetosa*	roots	soft pink with alum
Tansy *Tanacetum vulgare*	leaves	yellow/green with alum; bright lemon with tin

Sweet Candles and Incense

Bought candles are a little impersonal for a gift, but homemade ones are a pleasure to make and receive. They can reflect the season, convey an intimate message with their scent or colour, or simply match the recipient's favourite room. Making candles today is much simpler than it was for Grandma — wax, wicks, colourings and a wide variety of decorative moulds are all readily available from good craft shops or art supply stores.

Burning aromatic incense made from fragrant plant gums and spices is another very ancient method for scenting or purifying the home. In 1661, Stevenson adjured that: "One should be sure night and morning to perfume the house with angelica seeds, burnt in a fire-pan or chafing dish of coales". In 1719, a certain Mrs Mary Ealse, Chief Confectioner to the doughty Queen Anne, recorded the method she had devised for preparing the "odoriferous parfume" preferred by her mistress: "Take 3 Spoonfuls of Perfect Rosemary and as much Sugar as a half a Walnut beaten into a small powder; all these boyle together in a Perfuming-pan upon hot Embers, with a few Coals". During times of plague, aromatics such as juniper, lavender and bay were all burned to combat infection; others, such as tansy and southernwood, were used to deter flies and fleas. A French provincial custom which continues today sees the farmers' wives carrying a "fire-pan" of heated, smoking cloves and cayenne, or other mixed spices, from room to room each day to freshen the air.

28

Honeysuckle Candles

Candle moulds
350 g/12 oz paraffin wax
35 g/1¼ oz stearin
6–10 drops honeysuckle essence

ground turmeric
30 g/1 oz honeysuckle flowers,
    dried
vegetable oil

Prepare the moulds according to the manufacturer's instructions. There will be 6–12 moulds in a set, depending on the size and shape of candle wanted. Melt wax in the top half of a double boiler over simmering water. Melt the stearin in a second double boiler and add it to the wax. Stir in honeysuckle essence and add enough turmeric powder to give the candles a rich, golden-yellow colour. Mould candles and allow to set. To decorate candles, keep a little of the wax aside. When candles are firm, re-melt reserved wax, paint the backs of the honeysuckle flowers and press firmly onto candle. Then heat a long tin half filled with clear paraffin wax and dip candles once or twice until a thin transparent glaze appears on the flowers. Leave to harden. To give candles a smooth, gleaming finish, polish them with cottonwool dipped in a mixture of vegetable oil and honeysuckle essence.

Spicy Rose Incense Pastilles

These are particularly appropriate in a musty sick room where the sweet aroma is much appreciated by the convalescent.

pinch each powdered
    frankincense, sandalwood
    and clove powder
200 g/7 oz charcoal
30 g/1 oz raspings of cascarilla
    or aromatic bark

110 g/3¾ oz gum benzoin
3 tsp gum tragacanth
few drops bergamot oil
1 tsp rose oil
rosewater

Grind dry ingredients together with a mortar and pestle, then add resins and oils. Blend thoroughly, adding a little rosewater if needed. Mould pastilles about 2.5 cm/1 in in diameter. *Note*: The charcoal will make the pastilles burn well enough to release the aroma; however, a pinch or two of saltpetre may be added to keep them burning longer.

Lavender Incense Sticks

Remove the flower heads from a handful of long stems of lavender and cover the stems in saltpetre. Allow to dry thoroughly. Stand dried stalks in a terracotta jar or enamel pot filled with sand, ensuring they do not fall against each other, and set them alight. The lavender stems will smoulder just like a stick of incense.

Rosemary Candles

Candle moulds
350 g/12 oz paraffin wax
50 g/1¾ oz dried rosemary
   leaves, snipped
35 g/1¼ oz stearin

vegetable oil
rosemary essence

Prepare moulds according to manufacturer's instructions. Melt paraffin wax in a double boiler over simmering water. Add dried rosemary leaves to wax, stirring constantly to ensure even distribution. Melt the stearin in a second double boiler and add it to the wax. Mould candles and allow to set. The resulting effect is pretty as well as richly aromatic, a translucent grey-green candle filled with the suspended herbs. Colouring is therefore optional. Finish the hardened candles by polishing with cottonwool dipped in a mixture of vegetable oil and rosemary essence.

Beeswax and Wild Thyme Candles

Using beeswax instead of, or in conjunction with, paraffin wax gives candles a rich, tawny-yellow colour. It also enhances the scent of the herbs used in the candle with its natural honeyed scent.

Candle moulds
350 g/12 oz paraffin wax
350 g/12 oz natural beeswax
50 g/1¾ oz wild thyme leaves,
*   dried*
65 g/2¼ oz stearin

pink or green dye concentrate
vegetable oil
thyme oil

Prepare moulds according to manufacturer's instructions. Combine paraffin wax and beeswax in a double boiler over simmering water. Add thyme leaves to wax, stirring constantly to ensure even distribution. In a separate double boiler, combine stearin and dye according to manufacturer's instructions (either as ready-prepared powder, or grated from a tablet of craft dye). Stir stearin mixture into wax, mix well and pour into moulds. Leave to harden. Finish as for Honeysuckle Candles, polishing each candle with cottonwool dipped in a mixture of vegetable oil and thyme oil.

ODIFEROUS CANDLES AGAINST VENOM AND PLAGUE — Take Labdanum three ounces, Storax ten drams, Benjamin six drammes, Frankincence an ounce and a half, Staechados two ounces, red Roses, cloves, of each three ounces, Citron Peele, Yellow Sanders, of each three drammes, Juniper berries halfe an ounce, Muske and Ambergreece, of each halfe a scruple: forme them into Candles with gum dragant dissolve in Rose water.

From *The Charitable Physician,* by Philibert Guibert, French Physician Regent (1639)

Mint and Pennyroyal Candles

Candle moulds
350 g/12 oz paraffin wax
2 tbsp dried pennyroyal, snipped
   to short lengths with scissors
35 g/1¼ oz stearin
green dye concentrate (only a
   little, enough to make a very
   cool, pale green)

6–10 drops peppermint essence,
   and more for finish
large, fresh, mint leaves, for
   decoration
vegetable oil

Prepare moulds according to manufacturer's instructions. Melt paraffin wax in a double boiler over simmering water. Add dried pennyroyal to wax, stirring constantly to ensure even distribution. In a separate double boiler, combine stearin, dye and peppermint essence. Stir stearin mixture into wax, mix well and pour into moulds. Leave to harden. Decorate candles by painting the backs of the reserved fresh mint leaves with a little re-melted wax and pressing them firmly into a pattern around each candle. "Iron" the leaves into place by smoothing the candle wax gently with a warmed, dry spoon. Then paint over the top with the reserved wax. Finish by polishing candles with cottonwool dipped in a mixture of vegetable oil and peppermint essence.

2
Food and Drink

Country Baking

The fresh, yeasty smell of Grandma's kitchen on baking day was guaranteed to have her family dropping everything to come in and sample her cooking! Nothing is more delicious than the smell of fresh bread baking. Herbs such as dill and caraway add characteristic flavour, as do poppy and sesame seeds. Either add chopped fresh herbs to the dough before baking, or brush the tops of loaves with a little aromatic oil such as sage or rosemary. Bread and biscuits were once baked on branches of scented plants, especially fennel, to flavour them. During medieval times, many herbs and vegetables, like turnips, angelica and potatoes, were dried and ground for use as flour instead of wheat. Vegetable-based savoury loaves, or breads enriched with cheese, make a most nutritious and tasty snack, or add edible flowers and fruit to lightly spiced cakes, muffins and biscuits for a pretty tea-time treat.

Breadmaking is an art, and it is difficult to give precise instructions as flours vary, some not absorbing as much liquid as others. Rising times also vary, depending on room temperature and humidity and the type of container used. Most excellent bakers bewail their early efforts, remembering loaves which refused to rise or went stale within hours. Don't despair — like most arts, it takes practice. A few hints worth remembering: always warm all ingredients, including the flour, to

34

room temperature; add more liquid to dough mixture if it is not binding together (liquid amounts indicated in recipes are usually bare minimums); always smooth a very fine film of oil over the dough when kneading it, to stop it cracking and to ensure elasticity; and brushing the tops of loaves with oil or beaten egg gives a very professional, glossy finish.

Honeysuckle and Saffron Tea Bread

This delicious tea bread is a beautiful golden colour. For a variation with added impact, cover the top of the bread with a simple vanilla or lemon icing and scatter crystallised honeysuckle flowers over it.

> *300 mL/10½ fl oz milk*
> *½ tsp saffron threads*
> *1½ tsp dried yeast*
> *2½ tbsp clear honey*
> *450 g/1 lb plain flour*
> *1 tsp mace*
>
> *½ cup honeysuckle flowers,*
>   *minced*
> *100 g/3½ oz butter, softened*
> *water*
> *100 g/3½ oz mixed candied*
>   *orange and lemon peel*

Lightly grease a 22 cm/9 in ring or circular cake tin and set aside. Heat milk, place saffron in a mixing bowl and pour warmed milk over. Leave milk and saffron mixture for half an hour then strain liquid and reheat, keeping tepid. Sprinkle yeast into milk and saffron mixture, add ½ tablespoon of honey and mix well; set aside till mixture froths. Combine flour, mace and honeysuckle flowers in another mixing bowl. Add butter and enough water to make mixture crumbly. Make a well in centre and pour in yeast liquid and rest of honey. Mix to form a soft dough then turn out onto floured board and knead for 10 minutes. Return to bowl, cover and leave in a warm place for 1 hour. Dough should approximately double. Then mix in orange and lemon peel, shape dough into a ball or sausage and place in tin. Cover and leave for a further 45 minutes to rise again. Bake at 200°C/400°F for 45-50 minutes or until bread springs back to the touch. Glaze with a little honey or icing as suggested above.

Buttermilk and Apricot Drop Scones with Honey

½ tsp oil
200 g/7 oz self-raising flour, sifted
50 g/1¾ oz butter
grated zest of 1 orange
50 g/1¾ oz dried apricots, finely chopped

15 g/½ oz sugar
60 mL/2 fl oz buttermilk
1½ tbsp sour cream
extra buttermilk
1 tsp sesame seeds

Preheat oven to 230⁰C/450⁰F. Lightly grease a baking sheet with the oil and set aside. Place flour in bowl and rub in butter till mixture is crumbly. Add zest, apricots and sugar, then mix in buttermilk and sour cream to form dough. Turn out onto a lightly floured surface and knead till quite smooth. Roll out to about 2.5 cm/1 in thickness and cut rounds, using decoratively fluted pastry cutter. Place on baking sheet, leaving plenty of space between, and brush with extra buttermilk, sprinkle with sesame seeds and bake for 8–10 minutes or until browned. Serve hot, spread with honey.

To Make A Drunken Loaf — Take a French Roll hot out of the Oven, rasp it, and pour a Pint of Red Wine upon it. Cover it close up for half an hour. Boil one Ounce of Mackarony in Water, 'till it is soft, and lay it upon a Sieve to drain. Then put the size of a Walnut of Butter into it, and as much Thick Cream as it will take. Then scrape in six Ounces of Pumasant Cheese [Parmesan Cheese], shake it about in your Tossing Pan, with the Mackarony, 'till it be like a fine Custard. Then pour it hot upon your Loaf; brown it with a Salamander* and serve it up. It is a pretty Dish for Supper.

From *The Experienced English Housekeeper* by Mrs Elizabeth Raffald (1805)
*   "Salamander" here, does not refer to a large lizard gambolling about in a hot fire but rather to a circular iron plate, heated to be red-hot, that was placed over a pie or pudding to brown the crust.

Pecan-Cherry Bread

2 tbsp butter
1 cup sugar
2 eggs, lightly beaten
¾ cup dark grape juice
zest of 2 oranges

2 cups plain flour
½ tsp sea salt
2 tsp baking powder
¾ cup chopped pecan nuts
1 cup dried red tart cherries

Lightly grease and flour a 25 cm/10 in bread tin and set aside. Cream butter and sugar together, add eggs, grape juice and orange zest. Sift flour, salt and baking powder and blend with creamed mixture. Stir in nuts and cherries. Pour batter into tin and bake at 180°C/350°F for 1 hour or until bread springs back to the touch.

Sweet Corn and Sesame Seed Biscuits

100 g/3½ oz millet
enough boiling water to cover
    millet
75 g/2½ oz butter
50 g/1¾ brown sugar
50 mL/1¾ fl oz clear honey
1 egg, beaten
100 g/3½ oz canned sweet corn
    kernels, well drained

175 g/6 oz wholemeal self-
    raising flour
1 tsp baking powder
30 g/1 oz dried apricots, finely
    chopped
finely grated zest of 1 orange
50 g/1¾ oz sesame seeds

Preheat oven to 200°C/400°F. Gently simmer millet in boiling water for about 20 minutes till fluffy. Drain and set aside. Lightly grease 2 baking trays and set aside. Melt butter, sugar and honey together in a saucepan and set aside. Combine egg and corn; set aside. Mix flour and baking powder in a bowl, then add millet, butter mixture and corn mixture, mixing thoroughly with a wooden spoon. Add apricots, orange zest and sesame seeds. Stir well. Shape spoonfuls of mixture into rounds and place on baking trays, allowing room to spread. Bake for 10-15 minutes or until golden-brown. Cool on trays then transfer to wire rack.

Carrot, Hazelnut and Herb Loaf

450 g/1 lb wholemeal plain
   flour
½ tsp salt
30 g/1 oz dried yeast
300 mL/½ pt warm water
raw sugar, pinch
50 g/1¾ oz chopped fresh herbs
   (parsley, chives, thyme,
   marjoram)
1 carrot, scrubbed and finely
   grated

1 small onion, skinned and
   finely chopped
1 tbsp chopped hazelnuts
100 g/3½ oz Cheddar cheese,
   grated
1 tsp mustard powder
cayenne pepper, pinch
black pepper, to taste

Grease and flour a large 30 cm/12 in bread tin and set aside. Warm flour and salt in slow, 150°C/300°F, oven for a few minutes only. Add yeast to water with a pinch of sugar and set aside till frothy. Add yeast liquid to flour and mix well. Add herbs, carrot, onion, hazelnuts, cheese, mustard powder, cayenne and black peppers, mixing well with wooden spoon. Turn out dough onto lightly floured board and knead well. Place in bread tin, cover with a dry cloth and set aside for 45 minutes to prove. (*Note*: this is a fairly solid and moist loaf and will not rise as dramatically as normal bread.) Preheat oven to 220°C/425°F and bake loaf for about 15 minutes then reduce heat to 180°C/350°F and cook for a further 30–45 minutes. Carefully turn out loaf onto warmed plate and serve with vegetable soup or on its own with cream cheese.

DAMPER — Self-raising Flour, water, salt. Mix ingredients into a stiff dough, mould into flat cakes, dust with dry flour, and cook in hot ashes, a camp oven or a brick oven. Test with a piece of wood (if it comes out clean the damper is done). If you have not self-raising flour, take to every pound of flour ½ a teaspoon of carbonate soda and 1 teaspoon of cream of tartar.

From *The CWA Cookery Book and Household Hints* (1936)

Caraway wygges

These spicy buns were very popular in the 18th century, when they were eaten with coffee at breakfast.

15 g/½ oz dried yeast	*pinch nutmeg*
225 mL/8 fl oz warmed milk	*½ tsp ground ginger*
450 g/1 lb wholemeal plain flour, sifted	*½ tsp allspice*
	2 tsp caraway seeds
60 g/2 oz brown sugar	*2 tbsp sweet sherry*
1 tsp sea salt	*1 egg, beaten*
125 g/4½ oz butter	*extra egg, beaten, for glaze*

Dissolve yeast in milk with a pinch of the sugar. Set aside in a warm place until mixture is frothy. Place flour, sugar and salt in a bowl, rub in butter and work mixture till crumbly. Add spices and caraway seeds and mix well. Make a well in centre and pour in yeast mixture, sherry and egg, mixing well. Turn mixture onto lightly floured surface and knead for 10 minutes. Return to bowl, cover and set aside to rise for 1 hour, or until dough doubles in size. Heat oven to 200ºC/400ºF. Knock down dough, knead again and roll out to about 2.5 cm/1 in thickness. Cut into desired shapes with sharp knife (should make approximately 16 squares, circles or diamonds) and place on floured baking sheet. Cover with cloth and leave to rise for 45 minutes. Brush the tops with the extra egg and bake for 15-20 minutes, or until golden-brown.

Pesto and Walnut Twist

Pesto
1 cup fresh basil
¼ cup parsley
¼ cup olive oil
1 garlic clove, peeled and
    crushed
pinch sea salt
¼ cup freshly grated Parmesan
    cheese

Dough
1½ tsp dried yeast
sugar, pinch

300 mL/10½ fl oz tepid water
225 g/8 oz plain flour
225 g/8 oz wholemeal plain
    flour
1 egg, beaten
1½ tbsp roasted walnuts,
    chopped
¼ cup packed, pitted, black
    Greek olives, chopped
    roughly
1 tsp milk
poppy seeds

Prepare pesto by blending basil, parsley, oil, garlic and salt in food processor till smooth. Stir through Parmesan and set aside.

Lightly oil a large loaf tin or tray. Sprinkle yeast and pinch of sugar into 150 ml/5¼ fl oz of tepid water and place in a warm place till frothy. Sift flours together and put in a warm place to heat through. Add yeast liquid, egg and about another 150 mL/5¼ fl oz of tepid water, or enough to work into a smooth dough. Turn onto lightly floured board and knead for 4-6 minutes. Place in a bowl, cover and leave to rise for half an hour, or until dough has doubled in size. Turn out dough again and knock down to remove all air bubbles. Knead for a further 5 minutes and set aside again for half an hour. Knock down and knead again till smooth, this time rolling, patting and stretching dough into a roughly rectangular shape. Spread 3 tablespoonfuls of the pesto on dough, then scatter layer of walnuts and olives and roll up tightly, like a Swiss roll. Place loaf in pan "seam" down and brush top with a little milk; sprinkle with poppy seeds. Bake at 230°C/450°F for 20-30 minutes or until loaf is golden. Place on rack to cool slightly and serve warm, with extra pesto, for best flavour.

> *Sit down and feed and welcome to our table*

BUSH SCONES — 1 lb self-raising flour, 1 cup of sour milk. Put flour in a bowl, add milk and mix quickly with knife blade. Turn onto floured board, knead quickly and cut shapes as required. Place on warm floured tray into hot oven 10 to 15 minutes. Wonderful made in a camp oven and eaten with lemon butter — home-made — and scalded cream.

From *Australian Early Settlers' Household Lore* compiled by Mrs L. Pescott, Ballarat Historical Park Association, Sovereign Hill (1977)

Soft Cinnamon and Pumpkin Seed Buns

75 g/2½ oz honey
200 mL/7 fl oz warm milk
30 g/1 oz dried yeast
675 g/1 lb 8 oz wholemeal flour
1 tsp salt
2–3 tsp cinnamon
50 g/1¾ oz pumpkin seeds,
  shelled and chopped

75 g/2½ oz walnuts, finely
  chopped
75 g/2½ oz raisins
4 eggs, beaten
75 g/2½ oz brown sugar
tbsp cinnamon and sugar mixed
extra egg, beaten

Lightly grease and flour a baking sheet and set aside. Dissolve 5 g/¼ oz honey in milk and sprinkle in yeast. Set aside in a warm place until mixture is frothy. In another bowl, mix together flour, salt, cinnamon, pumpkin seeds, walnuts and raisins. Make a well in the centre of the mixture and add yeast liquid, the rest of the honey and the eggs. Knead to a smooth dough for 5 minutes, adding extra flour if necessary. Place in a bowl, cover with a cloth and set aside for 1 hour or until mixture has doubled in size. Preheat oven to 200°C/400°F. Turn out dough and knock down again and roll out to about 1.25 cm/½ in thick. Sprinkle with brown sugar and extra cinnamon and sugar and then roll up, Swiss-roll style, from the long end. Cut into 12 slices and place on baking sheet close together. Brush with beaten egg, sprinkle with cinnamon and sugar, and leave in a warm place to prove for 30–45 minutes. Bake for about 20–25 minutes, until risen and golden-brown. Cool on rack and serve warm with sour cream.

Almond, Date and Fig Bread

75 g/2½ oz butter
100 g/3½ oz brown sugar
2 large eggs, beaten
50 g/1¾ oz chopped candied
    peel
225 g/8 oz plain flour
2½ tsp baking powder
½ tsp allspice
1½ tsp cinnamon powder

50 mL/1¾ fl oz sour cream
1 tbsp brandy
50 g/1¾ oz currants
75 g/2½ oz dried dates, stoned
    and minced
75 g/2½ oz dried figs, minced
50 g/1¾ oz almonds, chopped
    finely

Lightly grease and flour a 25 cm/10 in round cake tin and set aside. Preheat oven to 170ºC/335ºF. Cream butter and sugar, gradually adding eggs and candied peel. Sift flour, baking powder, allspice and cinnamon and add to creamed mixture. Add sour cream, brandy and then stir in currants, dates, figs and almonds. Spoon into prepared tin and bake in oven for 1–1½ hours. Cake is baked when it springs back to the touch or when a skewer is inserted and comes away clean. To serve, cut slices and butter lavishly.

Cheese and Chilli Challah

30 g/1 oz butter
150 mL/¼ pt water, warmed
10 g/⅓ oz dried yeast
raw sugar, pinch
450 g/1 lb plain flour
225 g/8 oz wholemeal plain
    flour
1 tsp sea salt
2 large jalapeño chillies, peeled,
    finely chopped and seeded

1 medium onion, skinned and
    minced
olive oil
1½ tsp cayenne pepper
50 g/1¾ oz Cheddar cheese,
    grated
freshly ground black pepper
1 egg yolk, beaten
poppy seeds

Melt butter in water and allow to cool slightly. Sprinkle dried yeast into warm water with pinch of sugar and set aside till frothy. Sift flours and salt into a bowl, make a well in the centre and add yeast liquid. Knead until smooth and elastic. Return to warmed, greased bowl and cover, leaving to rise for about 1 hour or until doubled in size. Sauté chillies and onion in a little olive oil over medium heat till tender; add cayenne pepper. Knead dough mixture again, mixing in cheese, black pepper and the chilli-onion mixture. Knead for a further 10 minutes (being careful not to rub eyes with hands as chillies will burn them). Divide into 3 pieces — 1 large, 1 medium and 1 small. Roll each into a long sausage and place them on a greased and floured baking sheet (largest first, then medium and then small) and "plait" them up into one shape. Cover and set aside again to rise in a warm place. Brush the whole loaf with beaten egg yolk and scatter thickly with poppy seeds. Bake in a hot oven, 220°C/425°F, for 15 minutes before reducing heat to 160°C/325°F and cooking for a further 45 minutes, or until loaf sounds hollow when knocked on the bottom. Cool on a wire rack.

POTATO AND LEMON CHEESECAKES — Take six ounces of potatoes, four ounces of lemon-peel, four ounces of sugar, four ounces of butter, boil the lemon-peel till tender, pare and scrape the potatoes, and boil them tender and bruise them; beat the lemon-peel with the sugar then beat all and mix all together very well and let it lie till cold: put crust in your pattipans, and fill them a little more than half full: bake them in a quick oven over half an hour, sift some double refin'd sugar on them as they go into the oven; this quantity will make a dozen small pattipans.

From *The Compleat Housewife* by E. Smith (1736)

Preserves, Jellies and Butters

The flavour and fragrance of flowers, leaves and sprigs of fresh herbs can be sealed into preserves to bring back memories of sunny days when the weather is poor. Fresh fruit, vegetables and herbs were not available all year round, so Grandma would bottle her harvest for use in autumn and winter. There are innumerable recipes for spicy country jams and sweet-scented jellies in the old books on cookery and domestic lore. Once made, few sights are prettier than the rows of jars lining the pantry windowsill, gleaming like jewels, just as they did in Grandma's era.

Suitable flowers to use include violet, borage, bergamot, lavender, rosemary, clove pink, sage, marigold petals and rose petals (with the tart white "heel" removed). Choose leaves such as mint, violet, bergamot and lemon balm, or spices such as aniseed and coriander to give extra tang to savoury or sweet preserves of apples, quinces and greengage plums. Apples have a naturally high pectin content and the green underripe "cooking" apples are generally preferred for making jams and jellies. Extra pectin, available from delicatessens, may be needed to set a mixture based on low pectin fruit, such as elderberries, guavas or oranges. Another tip is to always add a little lemon juice to your jam or jelly as it nears setting or "gel" point; this will help prevent discolouration.

Spicy Apple Jelly

This is delicious with roast pork or with cold meat salads.

1 kg/2¼ lb green Granny Smith
   apples
4 cinnamon sticks, flaked
2 tbsp whole cloves
½ tsp grated nutmeg
2 tbsp whole allspice berries

2 cups apple cider vinegar
1 tbsp lemon juice
5 cups white sugar
¼ cup dried orange peel

Chop apples roughly, cores and all, and place in a large, non-aluminium saucepan. Tie cinnamon sticks, whole cloves, grated nutmeg and allspice berries in a muslin cloth bag and add to pan with vinegar and lemon juice. Simmer until apples become pulpy then remove spice bag and place apple mixture in a jelly bag and leave to drip overnight into bowl. Measure liquid and add 1 cup of sugar to each cup of apple liquid. Bring to the boil until mixture becomes syrupy. Add orange peel, stirring constantly to keep it in suspension. Continue to boil; when mixture reaches gel point, spoon into heated sterile glass jars and cap securely.

PRESERVING PASSIONFRUIT — This is one of the most useful of our fruits, but most people make the mistake when using passionfruit in cooking, of boiling the seeds and juice. To retain the distinctive flavour of the passionfruit, these should never be raised to a temperature higher than 32ºC/90ºF — to bring them to boiling point kills the special flavour and hardens the seeds. Remove pulp from skins, adding sugar (which, of course, is in itself a preservative) in the proportion of 500 gr/1 lb of sugar to 6 dozen passionfruit. Stir over heat until sugar is dissolved, fill jars, and seal as with all bottled fruit.

From *The CWA Cookery Book and Household Hints* (1936)

Jellied Berry Relish

A zesty complement to cold meats and sandwiches, this is scrumptious with turkey or chicken.

2 tbsp gelatine
125 mL/4⅓ fl oz cold water
125 mL/4⅓ fl oz sherry
1 medium orange, peeled,
    chopped and seeded
2 punnets strawberries, washed
    and hulled

1 tbsp cranberry sauce
squeeze lemon juice
sugar, to taste
60 g/2 oz hazelnuts, finely
    chopped
1 tbsp grated orange zest

Combine gelatine and water in a blender jug and let stand. Heat sherry and add to mixture, processing at very low speed, just until gelatine dissolves. Add orange, strawberries, cranberry sauce and lemon juice and blend to purée. Add sugar, if desired. Add hazelnuts and orange zest and stir through gently. Decant into pretty glass serving dishes and chill until set, or spoon into warmed sterile jars and cap securely.

Pink Rose Petal Jam

This is delicious spread on melba toast or between the layers of a sponge cake.

6 cups white sugar
2 cups rosewater
1 cup orange flower water
1 cup water

24 sweet-scented pink roses
1 cup boiling water
2 tsp lemon juice

Combine sugar, rosewater, orange flower water and water in a non-aluminium saucepan; bring to the boil and cook rapidly until mixture is syrupy. Prepare roses by removing white "heel" from petals and place in a large china bowl with the cup of boiling water; stir gently. Add petals and liquid to boiling syrup, continuing to stir constantly. Boil for a further 30 minutes, pressing petals down into syrup. When petals are tender and syrup has clarified, add lemon juice and continue to boil again till gel point is reached. Spoon into sterile glass jars and cap securely.

MARMALADE FROM ROSE-HIPS — To every pound of hips allow half a pint of water; boil until the fruit is tender, then pass the pulp through a sieve which will keep back the seeds. To each pound of pulp add one pound of preserving sugar and boil until it Jellies.

From *Travels Round Our Village* by E. G. Hayden

Parsley Jelly

This is a traditional British favourite which provides a more subtle flavour than mint jelly. Other herbs, such as tarragon and bergamot, may be substituted for parsley.

6 generous handfuls parsley	*sugar*
zest of 1 lemon	*a few drops green food*
water	*colouring*
juice of 4 lemons	

Wash parsley, place in a saucepan with lemon zest and cover with water. Boil until parsley has turned pale yellow (about 1 hour). Strain liquid into a bowl, add lemon juice and then sugar, allowing 1 cup for every cup of liquid. Return to heat and boil until gel point is reached, adding green food colouring as desired. Pour into heated sterile jars, cap securely and refrigerate.

Tamarillo and Cinnamon Jam

1.5 kg/3 lb tamarillos
500 mL/17½ fl oz water
100 mL/3½ fl oz apple cider
  vinegar
¼ tsp powdered cinnamon

juice of 1–2 lemons
1 cinnamon stick
¼ tsp whole cloves
900 g/2 lb white sugar

Scald tamarillos, then drain and skin fruit; chop roughly. Combine in a large non-aluminium saucepan with water and vinegar, powdered cinnamon and lemon juice. Place cinnamon stick and cloves in a small muslin bag, tie securely and add to pan. Bring to the boil and simmer for half an hour, mashing against sides of pan. Remove muslin spice bag, bring to boil again and add sugar, stirring until dissolved; boil rapidly for 1 hour or until gel point is reached. Spoon into heated sterile jars and cap securely.

Plum, Orange and Marigold Compote

Try serving this tangy fruit compote with ice cream and thick custard.

1 orange
2 cups plums, stoned and
  chopped (reserve stones)
⅓ cup water

3 tbsp sugar
2 tbsp Grand Marnier
3 tbsp marigold petals

Wash orange and put through a mincer whole, discarding seeds only; place in heavy-based non-aluminium saucepan with plums, water and sugar. Place plum stones in a muslin bag, tie securely and place in pan too. Simmer for 1 hour or until mixture is pulpy though still a little chunky. Discard bag of plum stones. Stir through Grand Marnier and marigold petals and continue to cook for a few minutes. Spoon into heated sterile jars and cap securely.

Cherry and Rose Geranium Jam

150 mL/5 fl oz water
150 mL/5 fl oz dark grape juice
850 g/1¾ lb caster sugar
1.5 kg/3 lb morello cherries,
    stoned (reserve stones)

1 vanilla pod
3 generous handfuls rose
    geranium leaves
1–2 tbsp red rose petals
juice of ½ lemon

Combine water, grape juice and sugar over low heat and then bring to the boil. Add cherries and vanilla pod. Place rose geranium leaves, rose petals and cherry stones in a muslin bag, tie securely and add to boiling mixture; continue to cook for 15–20 minutes. Remove from heat, stir through lemon juice, cover and cool for 2½–3 hours. Return to heat and bring to boil again until gel point is reached. Remove pod and muslin bag, turn jam into heated sterile jars and cap securely.

Passionfruit Butter

This makes delicious tarts for afternoon tea, when the butter is used to fill baked pastry cases.

6–8 passionfruit
1 tbsp butter

2 eggs
250 g/9 oz sugar

Beat all ingredients together in a jug for 1 minute with a wooden spoon. Stand in a pan of boiling water and cook, stirring constantly, till all the butter is melted. Cook gently for another 15–20 minutes, stirring occasionally. Do not let it boil. Spoon into heated sterile jars and cap securely.

Bergamot and Quince Jelly

2 kg/4½ lb quinces
1 bunch bergamot leaves
water

white sugar
fresh bergamot leaves, to
garnish

Wash and chop quinces roughly, cores and all, and place in a large, non-aluminium saucepan. Add bergamot and water to cover, and simmer till pulpy. Strain mixture overnight through a muslin jelly bag. Measure and add 1 cup of sugar to each cup of liquid. Return to heat and bring to the boil, cooking till gel point is reached. Allow to cool slightly before pouring into heated, sterile glass jars. Place a bergamot leaf in the top of each jar, poking down slightly with a skewer so that it may be seen; cap securely.

Gingered Kumquat and Whisky Marmalade

This recipe keeps very well — it's an ideal choice for preparing Christmas gifts ahead of time.

24 firm, ripe kumquats
250 g/9 oz jellied or finely
*   chopped ginger*
3 tbsp powdered ginger

6 tbsp whisky
water
sugar

Wash kumquats thoroughly. Peel fruit, cutting peel in long fine strips; reserve pith. Cut fruit into chunks and place with peel in a large non-aluminium saucepan; reserve seeds. Place pith and seeds in a muslin bag, tie securely and place in saucepan with fruit peel, jellied ginger, powdered ginger and whisky. Add water to barely cover, place lid on saucepan and leave to soak overnight. Bring mixture to the boil and simmer till peel is tender. Reduce heat and cook till mixture is pulpy. Measure pulp and add 1 cup of sugar for every cup of pulp. Bring to the boil to dissolve sugar and cook until gel point is reached. Spoon into sterile glass jars and cap securely. *Tip:* When making marmalade, select only smooth, thin-skinned fruit. Fruit is best when there is next to no thickening of the rind at either blossom or stem ends. If this thickening is present, a slice should be rejected from either end to prevent bitterness.

Sweet Green Fig and Hazelnut Jam

1 kg/2¼ lb green figs, thinly
   sliced and chopped
1 lemon, thinly sliced
1 vanilla pod

water
3 cups sugar
1 cup hazelnuts, roughly
   chopped

Combine figs, lemon and vanilla pod in a large, non-aluminium saucepan, add a little water (only enough to stop mixture sticking to pan) and cook over low heat for 1 hour, stirring all the while. Add sugar and hazelnuts, and continue stirring over low heat for another 30–40 minutes or until gel point is reached. Remove vanilla pod. Spoon into heated sterile jars and cap securely.

To MAKE FAIRY BUTTER — Take the Yolks of four hard eggs, and half a Pound of Loaf Sugar beat and sifted, half a Pound of fresh Butter; bray them in a clean Bowl with two spoonfuls of Orange-flower Water; when it is well mixed, force it through the corner of a thin Canvas Strainer in little Heaps on a Plate. It is a very pretty Supper Dish.

From *The Receipt Book of Elizabeth Cleland* (1759)

PASSIONFRUIT JAM — Passionfruit, 1 cup sugar to each cup of pulp, ½ teaspoon lemon juice. Wipe the fruit well, cut into halves, and scoop out the seeds and the juice. Put the skins into a saucepan, add sufficient water to cover, and boil until the skins are quite tender. Then remove the fleshy part from the skins, and place in a pan with the seeds, juice, lemon juice, and sugar. Boil slowly till the jam sets. Bottle while hot, and cover closely.

From *The CWA Cookery Book and Household Hints* (1936)

Sage and Cider Jelly

2 kg/4½ lb green Granny Smith
  apples
1 large bunch fresh sage
apple cider

white wine vinegar
soft brown sugar
3 tbsp finely chopped fresh sage

Chop apples roughly, cores and all, and place in a large non-aluminium saucepan with bunch of fresh sage and a 50/50 mixture of apple cider and vinegar to cover. Simmer till mixture is pulpy and then strain overnight through a jelly bag. Measure liquid and add 1 cup brown sugar for each cup of liquid, return mixture to heat and boil till gel point is reached. Remove from heat and allow to cool and set slightly before stirring through finely chopped sage. Pour into heated sterile jars and cap securely.

Honeysuckle and Lemon Curd

This is delicious served with the Bush Scones (p. 41).

4 large lemons, zest and juice
1¼ cups white sugar
100 g/3½ oz butter

4 eggs, lightly beaten
handful honeysuckle flowers,
  chopped

Combine lemon zest, juice, sugar and butter in a double saucepan over low heat. Strain beaten eggs into lemon mixture, stirring all the while with a wooden spoon. Add handful of honeysuckle flowers. Continue stirring for 5-6 minutes or until mixture thickens and coats spoon. Strain through fine nylon sieve. Cool slightly and pour into sterile jars. Cover surface with wax discs (from speciality food stores) pressing into curd wax-side down. Cap immediately. Curd will thicken upon refrigeration. To serve, sprinkle with coarsely chopped candied lemon peel.

Herbed Grape Jelly with Currants

As well as being a spread for biscuits or cakes, try dissolving a spoonful of this jelly in hot water and using it as a cordial for soothing a sore throat.

1 tbsp fresh thyme leaves   *2 cups sugar*
1 L/1¾ pt dark grape juice   *150 g/5¼ oz currants*
500 mL/¾ pt white grape juice

Simmer thyme leaves and grape juices together for 5–10 minutes; strain. Combine liquid with sugar and bring to the boil, skimming to remove any scum from the surface, until volume is reduced to approximately two-thirds. Strain and pour into warmed sterile jars and allow to cool slightly. Stir 1 spoonful of currants through each jar as mixture nears setting point, so fruit will stay in suspension. Cap securely and wait until jelly is completely cold before serving.

Lillipilli Jam

A traditional Australian favourite and an easy way to harvest a tree overloaded with the distinctive pinky-mauve berries.

900 g/2 lb lillipillis *sugar*
water *lemon juice*

Wash fruit thoroughly, remove stems and discard any discoloured berries. Place fruit in a large non-aluminium saucepan and barely cover with cold water. Bring to the boil and cook for 50 minutes; cool slightly and strain through a jelly bag, pressing down well to extract as much juice as possible. Measure liquid and return to pan, adding one cup of sugar and the juice of half a lemon for each cup of lillipilli juice. Bring to the boil and cook rapidly until mixture reaches desired thickness. Spoon into heated sterile jars and cap securely.

Favourite Puddings

Seasoning the main course with herbs is nothing out of the ordinary, but how many of us are aware, as Grandma was, that certain flowers can add a sweet fragrance and delicate flavour to desserts. To make a delicious topping for fruit salad, add violet flowers or rose petals to a cup of sweetened thickened cream and infuse over a gentle heat for 20 minutes; strain. Stir in a teaspoon of brandy or grenadine syrup. Roses, violets and clove pinks may also be crystallised or frosted and used to decorate summer parfaits or sorbets. Soft desserts, such as grape jelly, creamy blancmanges and caramelised puddings are particularly ambrosial when garnished with a few delicate candied honeysuckle flowers or mint sprigs.

Tasty Pumpkin Pie

If gramma pumpkin is not available, other types of pumpkin will work just as well.

Filling
450 g/1 lb cooked gramma
    pumpkin
2 tsp butter
1 egg yolk
100 g/3½ oz brown sugar
juice and rind of 1 lemon
1 tsp cinnamon
¼ tsp nutmeg
2–3 sprigs lemon thyme, finely
    chopped

1 tbsp sultanas

Short crust pastry
225 g/8 oz plain flour
¼ tsp baking powder
1 egg yolk
1 tbsp water
dash lemon juice
110 g/3¾ oz butter

To make pastry — Sift flour and baking powder. Beat egg yolk, water and lemon juice together. Rub butter into flour very lightly till free from lumps. Add egg yolk mixture very slowly and make into a dry dough. Turn pastry onto a floured board and smooth into a round shape. Roll out lightly and line a 25–30 cm/10–12 in pie dish with half.
To make gramma filling — Steam gramma till tender, then mash with fork till smooth. Add butter, egg yolk, sugar, juice and rind of lemon, nutmeg, cinnamon, lemon thyme and sultanas, and mix well.

Spoon gramma filling into pastry case and cover with remaining half of pastry. Glaze with water and sugar. Bake in a hot oven, 220°C/425°F, until cooked. Sprinkle with icing sugar and serve with whipped cream.

Honeysuckle and Blueberry Pudding

2–3 punnets blueberries
1½ cups honeysuckle flowers,
    minced
50 g/1¾ oz caster sugar

¼ cup apple juice
6 slices fresh white bread, crusts
    removed

Combine berries and honeysuckle flowers in china bowl. Sprinkle with sugar, cover and refrigerate overnight. Place mixture in a saucepan, add apple juice and warm over a gentle heat. Tear 4 slices of the bread into quarters and press firmly around sides and base of china pudding bowl to form a "lining". Strain fruit and flower mixture and place in a bowl. Top with remaining slices of bread and drizzle reserved juice slowly and evenly over the top so it will soak through. Seal bowl with an inverted plate, pressing down firmly, then place a weight on top of the plate and refrigerate overnight. To serve, run the wetted point of a knife around the edge of the dish before turning out onto a chilled plate. Serve with a dollop of natural yoghurt sprinkled with cinnamon sugar, or with plain whipped cream.

A FLOWER-PUDDING — Mince cowslip flowers, clove gillyflowers, rose petals and spinach of each a handful, take a slice of Manchet (white bread) and scald it with cream. Add a pound of blanch'd Almonds pounded small with Rose-water, a quarter of a Pound of Dates, sliced and cut small, the yolks of three eggs, a handful of Currants, and sweeten all with Sugar. When boiled pour Rose-water over and scrape Sugar on, then serve up.

From *The Receipt Book of John Nott,* Cook to the Duke of Bolton (1723)

Shoo Fly Pie and Apple Pan Dowdy

> Shoo fly pie and apple pan dowdy
> Make your eyes light up
> And your stomach say "Howdy!"
> Shoo fly pie and apple pan dowdy
> I never get enough
> Of that wonderful stuff.

So runs a funny old song my mother used to sing. Shoo Fly Pie is so-called because after a Pennsylvanian Dutch housewife had baked one, she would leave it out to cool and then would have to shoo away the flies which were very partial to the molasses in the recipe. I don't know how Apple Pan Dowdy got its name, but both are delicious.

Shoo Fly Pie

1 unbaked pie shell (see
    Gramma Pumpkin Pie, Short
    Crust Pastry p.56)

Crumb mixture
¼ cup butter
1½ cups plain flour
1 cup brown sugar

Filling
¾ tsp baking soda
punch each nutmeg, ginger,
    cinnamon and cloves
¼ tsp salt
¾ cup molasses
¾ cup hot water

To make crumb mixture — work butter, flour and sugar together to form a crumble and set aside.

To make filling — combine dry ingredients and molasses; add hot water. Place alternate layers of crumb mixture and molasses liquid into unbaked pie shell, with crumbs forming first (bottom) and last (top) layers. Bake at 225⁰C/440⁰F for 15 minutes before reducing heat to 180⁰C/350⁰F and cook for a further 20 minutes or until done.

Apple Pan Dowdy

4 Granny Smith apples
grated zest of 1 lemon
¼ cup brown sugar
1 cup plain flour
1 tsp baking powder

pinch each allspice and vanilla
¼ cup milk
60 g/2 oz melted butter
½ cup sugar
1 egg

Peel, core and slice apples and place in the bottom of a deep, buttered 10 cm/4 in square or round baking dish. Sprinkle grated lemon rind and sugar over apples. Make batter mixture by whisking together all remaining ingredients and pour over apples. Bake in a moderate oven, 190⁰C/375⁰F, for approximately 35-40 minutes. To serve, invert onto dish and drizzle custard over.

Traditional Christmas Pudding

Christmas is a time for giving as well as entertaining. Why not make several of these traditional British puddings and offer them as gifts to friends as Grandma would have done.

225 g/8 oz raisins
225 g/8 oz sultanas
225 g/8 oz currants
225 g/8 oz butter
225 g/8 oz brown sugar
zest of 1 lemon
1 grated nutmeg
5 eggs, beaten

225 g/8 oz plain flour
1 tsp allspice
½ tsp each cinnamon,
* and cloves*
1 tsp bicarbonate of soda
pinch salt
110 g/3¾ oz breadcrumbs
110 mL/3¾ fl oz brandy

Pick over and prepare fruit, removing stalks or discoloured parts. Cream butter and sugar and add lemon zest and nutmeg. Gradually add beaten eggs, then fruit, then flour, spices, soda and salt, all well sifted together. Add crumbs and brandy and mix well. Tie mixture in a well-floured pudding cloth, allowing room for the pudding to swell. Boil constantly for 6–8 hours. Serve hot or cold with traditional hard sauce or a boiled custard.

Hard Sauce

¼ cup rum
1 cup sugar

50 g/1¾ oz butter
⅓ cup water

Combine rum, sugar and butter with water and cook over a low heat, stirring, until sugar is dissolved and sauce is hot. Serve hot or cold. Makes about 1½ cups.

Make hunger thy sauce, as a medicine for good health

Rhubarb and Orange Fool with Bergamot

Served garnished with red bergamot flowerheads, this food is a delicious dessert. It is also worth remembering as a nourishing restorative for a patient with a sore throat.

450 g/1 lb rhubarb
4 tbsp bergamot leaves,
*   chopped*
grated rind and juice of 2
*   medium oranges*
4 tbsp clear honey
vanilla pod

200 mL/7 fl oz milk
4 egg yolks, whisked
200 mL/7 fl oz thickened
*   (double) cream*
bergamot flowers for
*   decoration, if desired*

Chop rhubarb roughly and place in a non-aluminium saucepan with bergamot, orange juice and rind, and honey. Cover and cook over very low heat for 10-15 minutes or until rhubarb is tender and honey has melted. Purée mixture and refrigerate. Place vanilla pod and milk in a double saucepan and cook gently for 5–7 minutes, allowing mixture to simmer but not boil. Remove vanilla pod, reduce heat and add egg yolks to warm milk, whisking mixture together over low heat until it thickens and becomes custardy. Allow to cool, whip cream and fold through rhubarb mixture, then lightly fold custard through, too. Spoon fool into serving dish and chill before serving.

TO MAKE TARTS CALLED TAFFITY TARTS — First wet your paste with Butter and cold water and roule it very thin, also then lay them in layers and between every lay of apples strew some sugar and some lemond pill, cut very small. If you please, put some Fennel seed to them; then put them into a stoak hot oven, and let them stand an houre in or more, then take them out and take Rose-water and Butter beaten together and wash them over with the same and strew fine sugar upon them, then put them into the oven againe, let them stand a little while and take them out.

From *The Compleat Cook* (1655)

Peach and Pink Rose Petal Ice Cream

Decorated with crystallised rose petals and slices of fresh peaches, this is a delicious finale for that special dinner.

250 g/9 oz canned peaches, strained
2 cups pink rose petals, minced, with white "heels" removed
4 egg yolks
50 g/1¾ oz caster sugar
350 mL/12 fl oz thickened (double) cream
rosewater

Purée peaches to obtain approximately 250 mL/9 fl oz liquidised fruit. Combine peaches purée with rose petals over low heat and simmer for 30 minutes. In a double boiler, whisk egg yolks and sugar together, adding cream gradually until mixture forms a custardy coating on the back of a metal spoon. Remove from heat and allow to cool slightly before folding in peach mixture. You may wish to add a few drops of rosewater to enhance flavour and scent. Pour mixture into metal bowl and chill until it begins to freeze. Remove from freezer. Beat vigorously until smooth and creamy. Pour into tray or decorative ring mould and freeze.

- Prepare a summer dessert platter, skewering soft jubes and small chunks of fruit with lavender stems.

- Infuse scented flowers, such as honeysuckle, primroses, or clove pinks, in warmed cream. Use strained cream to make custards, rice puddings and syllabubs. Whipped and hot, it makes a luscious topping for fruit pies and scones.

- Flower sugar, made by storing scented flowers in the sugar canister, adds a new dimension to sweet dishes. It is especially lovely when dusted over summer fruits still fresh with dew. Substitute flower sugar for ordinary sugar when preparing creamy desserts and add it to whipped cream or plain boiled custard.

- Whether served to cleanse the palate between courses or as a summertime dessert, a herb or flower sorbet is a delicious alternative. Rosemary sorbet is particularly refreshing while scoops of mauve and pink rose and lavender sorbets make an eyecatching centrepiece, displayed in a chilled silver tureen. The basic method for any sorbet is:

2 cups sugar
5 cups water or 2¹/₂ cups
* water and 2¹/₂ cups*
* champagne*

¹/₄ cup herbs or flowers,
* chopped*
1 large egg white

Dissolve sugar in liquid, bring to the boil then infuse herbs or flowers for 30 minutes. Strain and pour into a metal freezer tray. Chill until mixture begins to freeze, then fold through whisked egg white. Freeze again till firm.

Old-fashioned Sweets

The first sweetmeats were pieces of candied citrus fruit peel. Later, as sugar's preserving qualities became better known, other aromatic herbs and flowers were candied and crystallised, too. Mint and ginger were natural herbs for flavouring sweets, as were roses, lavender, lemon balm and lemon verbena. Even the extremely aromatic bay, clove pink, rosemary, anise, caraway, coriander, thyme and lavender can be used for sweets and candies, or crystallised and used as garnishes and decorations. "Lozinges" made from red roses, "dry suckets" of angelica, "wet suckets" of marshmallow stalks and fruit-based jubes flavoured with herbs like horehound or aniseed, were all used primarily as medicine, being prescribed for sore throats, indigestion and even as aphrodisiacs! Perhaps a remnant of this use is seen in the customary gift of chocolate between lovers — the time-honoured "sweets to the sweet" — not that sweets were ever just for their sole indulgence. For generations, small children have clustered devotedly around Grandma's skirts as she cooked wonderful foaming honeycomb, delicious chewy fudge or nougat, peanut brittle and glossy crimson toffee apples. Sometimes, if they were very good, adults were allowed to share, too. . .

CANDIED HONEY — Boil some horehound till the juice is extracted. Boil up some sugar to a feather height, add your juice to the sugar, and let it boil till it is again the same height. Stir it till it begins to grow thick, then pour it on to a dish and dust it with sugar and when fairly cool cut into squares. Excellent sweetmeat for colds and coughs.

From *The Family Herbal* by R. Thornton (1810)

Sinfully Rich Rum Balls

1 cup hazelnuts, roughly ground
1 cup chocolate wafer biscuit
  crumbs
1 cup soft brown sugar
1½ tbsp corn syrup or light
  treacle

¼ cup dark rum
cocoa powder for dusting
icing sugar
coconut

Grind together nuts and biscuit crumbs in a food processor. In a large bowl, work nut mixture thoroughly into sugar, syrup and rum to form firm paste. Add extra rum or biscuit crumbs until you have a texture that can be rolled into firm, bite-sized balls. Dust with cocoa and then roll alternate balls in icing sugar and coconut. Store in an airtight container in a cool place. Freezes well.

Toffee Apples

3 cups white sugar
1 cup water
pinch cream of tartar
60 g/2 oz butter
2 tsp apple cider vinegar

cochineal
1 kg/2¼ lb small bright red
  apples (Red Delicious, Jonathans
  or Christmas apples are best)

Combine sugar, water, cream of tartar, butter and vinegar in a heavy-based saucepan and bring to the boil, stirring constantly. When toffee reaches "hard crack" stage (snaps and is very brittle when a droplet is put in glass of cold water), stir through enough cochineal to make mixture go rosy-red. Remove pot from high heat and either place on soft burner or into larger pot of hot water so toffee does not start to set. Wash and dry apples thoroughly and stick wooden skewers into top of each apple before dipping and twirling into toffee mixture. Stand apples on an oiled marble slab or baking sheet and allow to set.

Orange and Port Wine Jubes

450 g/1 lb sugar
2 tbsp orange rind, finely grated
1 tsp grated nutmeg
150 mL/¼ pt port
juice of 2 oranges

water, if necessary
50 g/1¾ oz gelatine
lemon juice
icing sugar
moulds

Combine sugar, orange rind and nutmeg. Mix port and orange juice in a jug, adding enough water to make 250 mL/9 fl oz. Reserve half the liquid. Sprinkle gelatine over remaining liquid and leave for half an hour. Combine with reserved liquid, sugar, orange rind and nutmeg and squeeze of lemon juice, to taste, in a non-aluminium saucepan over low heat and gradually bring to the boil. Allow to simmer until mixture becomes thicker before pouring into slightly moistened moulds. Chill to set and dust lightly with icing sugar. Top each jube with a crystallised flower and serve on a bed of glossy green citrus leaves.

Caraway and Ginger Butterscotch

200 g/7 oz butter
425 g/15 oz demerara sugar
juice of ½ orange

1½ tbsp caraway seeds, crushed
2 tsp powdered ginger

Melt butter over low heat in an iron-based saucepan. Add sugar and orange juice and stir till sugar has dissolved. Boil rapidly until setting point is reached (a droplet should crack when placed in a glass of cold water). Stir caraway and ginger through carefully, then pour into a buttered slice tin or shallow-rimmed baking sheet. Using point of a sharp knife, mark the mixture into squares and allow to cool before snapping squares apart and storing in an airtight jar.

Divinity Fudge

2 cups white sugar
½ cup water
1 tbsp powdered glucose

4–5 egg whites
½ cup chopped walnuts
½ cup chopped jellied ginger

Stir sugar, water and glucose together over low heat till clear. Beat egg whites till stiff peaks form. Bring syrup to boil and boil for 10 minutes. To test syrup, drop a piece in a glass of cold water — if it cracks, it is ready. Pour syrup very slowly onto beaten egg whites, holding saucepan with one hand and beating syrup in with the other while pouring. When syrup is all combined, add nuts and ginger; stir once or twice more and pour into buttered slice tray. Allow to set in cool place.

Aniseed Toffee

350 g/12 oz sugar
2½ tbsp honey
1½ tbsp cold water

110 g/3¾ oz butter
1 tbsp crushed aniseed
pinch allspice

Mix all ingredients in a heavy-based saucepan and bring to the boil. Cook for 10 minutes, or until "hard crack" stage — when a droplet placed in cold water will harden — is reached. Spread over an oiled, rimmed baking sheet. Mark into squares with the tip of a sharp knife and allow to cool. Snap squares apart and store in an airtight jar.

Crystallised Violets

The violets most commonly used in cooking are the sweetest Parma variety.

150 g/5 ¼ oz Parma violets   *caster sugar*
1–2 egg whites, lightly whisked

Using a small soft paint brush, or make-up brush, paint violets with egg white. Carefully dip flowers in the sugar, sprinkling a little extra over them where you have held them to ensure an even coating. Place violets on greaseproof paper spread on a wire rack and leave in a warm place to dry until they become brittle. Turn them occasionally so they dry evenly. Use to decorate sweet creamy desserts or cakes. Crystallised violets may be stored in an airtight container on absorbent paper for up to a week before use.

To Make Violet Cakes — Wet double refin'd Sugar, and boil it, till it is almost come to Sugar again; then put into it Juice of Violets, put in Juice of Lemons this will make them look red; if you put in Juice and Water it will make them look Green. If you will have them all and blanched almond and a few crums of bread and a little faire water and a pinte of Rose-water and mingle altogether and make it not too thin and frie it in oyl and so serve it in.

From *The Good Housewife's Handmaid* (1588)

Honeycomb

275 mL/9½ fl oz water
900 g/2 lb white sugar
225 g/8 oz powdered glucose

2 tsps bicarbonate of soda,
    sifted

Combine water, sugar and glucose in a heavy-based non-aluminium saucepan and bring to the boil. Remove from heat and quickly whisk through bicarbonate of soda, stirring rapidly till soda no longer rises to surface. Pour into well-buttered deep tins and allow to set. (*Tip:* pouring the mixture from as high as possible will help aerate it — even having the tins on the floor and pouring from the top of the kitchen table is a good idea!) Snap into pieces when cold.

Chocolate Macaroons

110 g/3¾ oz desiccated coconut
100 g/3½ oz almonds, finely
    chopped
100 g/3½ oz sweet dark
    chocolate, coarsely grated

225 g/8 oz caster sugar
3–4 egg whites

Combine coconut, almonds, chocolate and sugar; mix well. Beat egg whites to form stiff peaks and add to coconut mixture, beating to form a thick, pasty mixture. Place rounded teaspoonfuls onto a well-buttered baking sheet and bake in a slow to moderate oven, around 180ºC/350ºF, till firm.

Peppermint Chestnut Truffles

200 g/7 oz sweetened
   condensed milk
250 g/9 oz dark cooking
   chocolate, roughly grated
1 tbsp brandy
60 g/2 oz ground chestnuts

2 tbsp fresh mint, finely minced
1/2 tsp vanilla extract
few drops peppermint essence
crystallised mint leaves to
   decorate

Combine milk and chocolate in a double boiler over low heat until melted together. Stir through brandy, ground chestnuts, mint, vanilla and peppermint essence and mix thoroughly. Spoon mixture into a piping bag with small fluted nozzle and pipe into pretty paper or foil cases. Top each truffle with a pair of crystallised mint leaves, set in a butterfly shape.

Spiced Peanut Brittle

225 mL/8 fl oz water
675 g/1⅓ lb white sugar
½ tsp cream of tartar
60 g/2 oz butter
375 g/13 oz finely chopped
   peanuts

1 tsp bicarbonate of soda
pinch salt
1 tbsp crushed coriander seeds
1 tbsp powdered cumin

Combine water, sugar and cream of tartar in a heavy-based saucepan and bring to the boil. Stir in butter and chopped peanuts. Add bicarbonate of soda and salt, continuing to stir gently. Simmer steadily until a droplet placed in cold water becomes immediately hard. Stir in coriander and cumin. Pour into a buttered fudge tray or well-oiled baking sheet, mark into squares with sharp knife and allow to set. When cool, store in an airtight jar.

Spirited Occasions

Mead, metheglin and ale are thought to be the first alcoholic drinks prepared by humans. Traces of the different herbs, berries and flowers used to preserve and flavour these drinks have been found at ancient burial sites dating back to the Bronze Age. Hops have been used in Europe as a preservative and to add a bitter tang to beer for many centuries. The Middle Ages saw ale enriched with butter, eggs and many spices being used as a fortifying medicine, especially for the aged, and nursing mothers. Spicy mulled wines and punches, served piping hot, are still a popular winter drink in many countries.

Early wines were usually thin and vinegary, so strong-tasting herbs like balm and juniper and whole or ground spices were used to mask the flavour. As home wine-making became more popular during the seventeenth and eighteenth centuries, soft fruits, like blackberries and elderberries, the flowers of field and hedgerow, like cowslips and clary sage, and even the products of the vegetable

70

patch, like potatoes and turnips, were all used. Given the chemical additives so many of our modern-day wines and beers are subjected to, it is unsurprising that the home-style brews of Grandma's day are becoming popular once more.

Blackcurrant Brandy

Drink this delicious and unusual liqueur as an after-dinner digestive, or experiment with using it as a mixer, for example, in champagne cocktails.

100 g/3½ oz blackcurrants
4–6 blackcurrant leaves

2 tbsp caster sugar
400 mL/14 fl oz good quality brandy

Pack blackcurrants and leaves into a large 750 mL/1¼ pt bottle or preserving jar. Stir sugar into brandy until it has been dissolved, then pour over blackcurrant mixture. Seal jar and store in a cool dark place for several months, shaking it occasionally to ensure berries are evenly covered. The longer you leave the brandy, the stronger and sweeter its taste will become.

APPLE DRINK WITH SUGAR, HONEY, ETC — A very pleasant drink is made of Apples, Thus: — Boil sliced Apples in water to make the water strong of Apples, as when you drink it for coolness and pleasure. Sweeten it with Sugar to your taste, such a quantity of sliced apples as would make so much water strong enough of apples, and then bottle it up close for three or four months. There will come a thick mother at the top, which being taken off, all the rest will be very clear, and quick and pleasant to the taste, beyond any cider. It will be the better to most taste, if you put a very little Rosemary into the Liquor, when you boil it and a little Limon peel into each bottle, when you bottle it up.

From *The Closet of Sir Kenelm Digby Opened* (1699)

Mulled Claret

1 tsp cloves
1 cinnamon stick
½ tsp grated nutmeg
zest of ½ lemon
juice and zest of 1 orange

water
750 mL/1¼ pts claret
375 mL/13 fl oz sherry
sugar, to taste

Place spices and citrus zest in a large non-aluminium saucepan and barely cover with water. Simmer for 35-40 minutes, then strain and add liquid to claret, sherry and orange juice. Mix well in punchbowl, adding a little sugar if desired.

Spiced Whisky

Even the purists who believe good whisky should not be tampered with will be tempted by this aromatic recipe! It stores indefinitely and is ideal as a Christmas gift.

750 mL/1¼ pts good quality
    whisky
a piece of bruised ginger root
1 thinly sliced orange

1 thinly sliced lemon
1 tsp ground ginger
1 tbsp caraway seeds
250 g/9 oz soft brown sugar

Place all ingredients in a wide-mouthed jar or earthen crock and mix well. Cork firmly. Store in a warm dry place for 2–4 weeks, shaking jar regularly. Strain and re-bottle.

Orange and Lemon Liqueur

Liqueurs like this were once regarded as medicines because of their warming, stimulating effect. You might like to try it drizzled over fruit or creamy, lemon-based desserts.

1 cup dried lemon verbena
1 cup dried orange mint
1 cup dried orange zest (not pith)
2 tbsp whole cloves, crushed
1 15 cm/6 in cinnamon stick, crushed

2 tbsp lemon grass, crushed
500 mL/17½ fl oz alcohol, preferably vodka
200 g/7 oz white sugar
300 mL/½ pt water

Pack all herbs and spices into a sterile wide-mouthed jar. Warm alcohol slightly and pour over mixture. Seal jar securely and store in a warm dry place for 6–8 weeks, shaking gently every day or so. Dissolve sugar in water. Strain liquor from herb mixture, pressing down well so full flavour is obtained. Combine syrup and liqueur and pour into sterile bottles; cap securely.

ORANGE SHRUB — Break a hundred pounds of loaf sugar into small pieces, put it into twenty gallons of water, boil it till the sugar is melted, skim it well, and put it in a tub to cool; when cold, put it into a cask, with thirty gallons of good Jamaica Rum, and fifteen gallons of orange juice (mind to strain all the seeds out of the juice), mix them well together, then beat up the whites of six eggs very well, stir them well in, let it stand a week to fine, and then draw it off for use. By the same rules you may make any quantity you want.

From *The New Art of Cookery* by Richard Briggs, many years Cook at the Globe Tavern, Fleet Street, The White Hart Tavern, Holborn, and at the Temple Coffee House (1788)

Rose Petal and Woodruff Liqueur

Woodruff, with its aromatic taste, was one of the first herbs used to flavour wine.

100 g/3½ oz red rose petals,
   with white "heels" removed
12 sprigs woodruff
5 thin orange slices

500 mL/17½ fl oz alcohol,
   preferably vodka
200 g/7 oz white sugar
300 mL/½ pt water

Gently bruise petals, combine with woodruff and orange slices and pack firmly into wide-mouthed jar. Warm alcohol slightly and pour over. Seal jar securely and store in a warm dark place for 6–8 weeks, shaking jar gently every day or so. Strain liquor from petal and herb mixture, pressing down thoroughly to obtain maximum flavour. Make a syrup with the sugar and water and blend with the liquor; store in sterile bottle and cork firmly.

Strawberry Ratafia

2 punnets strawberries, with
   stems retained
500 mL/17½ fl oz Madeira wine
100 mL/ 3½ fl oz brandy

250 g/9 oz crushed barley sugar
1 vanilla pod
1 tsp coriander seeds
1 tsp sweet cicely seeds, bruised

Place all ingredients in a sterile glass preserving jar (or use a traditional stone container, if you have one) and seal. Store in a warm dry place for 4–6 weeks to ensure thorough steeping. Strain liquor from fruit mixture, pressing down well to obtain maximum flavour, and re-bottle.

Raspberry Vodka

The vodka which remains after making this recipe will be a pretty blush-pink. It may be decanted into another bottle and served as an aperitif or given away as a gift.

3 punnets raspberries
2 lemons, thinly sliced

700 g/1½ lb caster sugar
1.5 L/2½ pts vodka

Place raspberries and lemons in a large china bowl. Sprinkle liberally with sugar and chill overnight. Pack sweetened fruit into a wide-mouthed sterile glass preserving jar, cover with vodka and cap securely. Store in a cool dry place for 2–3 months, turning regularly so fruit remains evenly submerged. The berries shrink a little and should be strained off along with the lemon slices.

WINE FOR THE GODS — Take two great Lemons, peel them and cut them with two Pippens, pared and sliced like your lemons, put all this into a dish with three quarters of a pound of sugar in powder, a pint of Burgundy Wine, six cloves, a little orange-flower water. Cover this up and let it steep two or three hours then pass it through a bag as you do Hypocras and it will be most excellent.

From *A Perfect School of Instructions for Officers of the Month* by Giles Rose, one of the Master Cooks to Charles II (1682)

Honeysuckle Syllabub

Syllabubs originated in England but were perfected by the early American settlers who would serve them, topped with frothy cream and spices, as a Christmas beverage.

50 g/1¾ oz honeysuckle flowers
2 cups milk
2 cups thickened (double) cream
½ cup sherry

¼ cup white sugar
dash nutmeg
crystallised honeysuckle flowers,
 as garnish

Lightly bruise honeysuckle flowers and pour milk over. Cover and leave to infuse for 30 minutes. Strain off liquid, pressing down well on the flowers. Beat honeysuckle-flavoured milk with cream, sherry and sugar until sugar has dissolved and mixture is fluffy. Top each serving with honeysuckle flowers and a sprinkle of nutmeg. Serve immediately.

Hot Clove Pink Punch

The old country name for clove pinks was "sops-in-wine", referring to their frequent use in flavouring beverages such as this one.

zest of 1 orange	½ tsp nutmeg
1 tsp cloves	a piece of bruised root ginger
1 cinnamon stick	750 mL/1¼ pts claret or port
3 cardamom pods, crushed	50 g/1¾ oz raisins
1 tsp coriander	sugar, to taste
50 g/1¾ oz clove pink petals	

Put all ingredients, except wine and raisins, into a non-aluminium saucepan and barely cover with water. Simmer over low heat for 45 minutes–1 hour. Strain and add wine or port and raisins to liquid. Sweeten to taste and return to heat, but do not allow to boil. Serve immediately.

APRICOT WINE — Take twelve pounds of ripe Apricots, stone and pare them fine, put six pounds of good Sugar into seven quarts of water, boil them together and as the scum rises take it off, and when it has been well scummed, slip in the Apricots, and boil them till they become tender, then take them out, and if you please you may put in a Sprig or two of flowered Clary, and let it have a boil or two more, and when it is cold Bottle it up, and in six months it will be fit for drinking; but the longer it is kept the better it will be, for it will hold good for two years and more. After it has been Bottled a Week, you should try if there be any settlement, and if so, pour the liquor off into fresh Bottle, which may be afterwards separated again as it grows fine. The Apricots that are taken out may be made into marmalade, and will be very good for present spending; but will not keep long, unless they be used in Preserving.

From *M.S. Book of Receipts* by Charles Thomas Newington (1719)

3
Herbs and Spices

Freshly Minted

Mints have been used as strewing herbs for centuries, and they were also one of the tithing herbs in the Bible. In England, the leaves were scattered over church pews and through great halls to refresh the senses and repel vermin. Mice and rats hate the scent of mint, so it was always grown near food crops to deter them. In houses oil-soaked rags were used to stop up any holes found. Bees, on the other hand, love mint, and it was once customary to rub it on the inside of hives.

There are many different varieties within this group of aromatic herbs and they have been valued since ancient times. The most commonly available are: apple mint, eau-de-cologne mint, pennyroyal, peppermint, pineapple mint, spearmint and Corsican mint. Greeks and Romans crowned themselves with peppermint at banquets and placed bunches on tables. In fact, Roman matrons sucked on pastilles made of chopped mint and honey to disguise the fact that they had been drinking wine. Had they been found out, the punishment was death, for only men and gods were supposed to imbibe.

The Romans also polished their dining tables with mint, both to enhance the timber and to stimulate the appetite. The famous English herbalist, Nicholas Culpeper, obviously agreed with this Classical custom when he wrote: "The smell of mint doth stir up the minde and the taste to a greedy desire for meate". Mints are strongly associated with the culinary arts, being used traditionally as a relish with roast meats, especially lamb, and as a flavouring agent for commercial alcoholic drinks, notably Chartreuse and Benedictine liqueurs. Mint julep is a cocktail based on Bourbon whiskey and mint, which is very popular in America.

On blazingly hot summer days, a thirst-quenching and refreshing spritzer can be made from aerated mineral water, freshly squeezed lime juice, finely chopped mint and lots of ice. There are also many delicious punches that can be made with the basic ingredients of fruit juice and mint.

Mint Sugar

Simply add mint leaves to caster sugar (apple mint, spearmint and bergamot mint are the most aromatic). Put the mixture into a tightly lidded jar and store in a cool, dark place for at least three weeks, by which time the leaves will have dried and their essential oils will be incorporated into the sugar. Use the minty sugar for decorating cakes and to sprinkle on baked egg custards or creamy chocolate desserts. It can also be used to sweeten cool drinks in summer.

Apple Mint Jelly

6 Granny Smith apples
water
sugar

2 cups apple mint leaves,
chopped

Wash and quarter apples and place in a large non-aluminium saucepan with barely enough water to cover them. Cook until fruit is pulpy and soft. Strain this pulp overnight through a muslin jelly bag. For each cup of liquid obtained, add 1 cup of sugar and cook, with chopped apple mint, until mixture reaches gel point. Spoon jelly into clean, sterile jars and cap securely. *Note:* Stir the mint through the jelly often as it is coming to setting point, so it is evenly distributed.

Vegetable Bake with Mint and Yoghurt

The mint gives a fresh taste and aroma to this winter dish that everyone will enjoy. Adding half a tablespoonful of lightly crushed green peppercorns to the vegetables will add spice.

1 small eggplant (aubergine) sliced

sea salt

juice of 1 lemon

1 tbsp olive oil

8 tbsp chopped mint

1 tsp ground cumin

1 garlic clove, crushed

black pepper, to taste

1 butter (yellow) capsicum, sliced lengthwise

2–3 zucchinis (courgettes), sliced lengthwise

2 baby golden squash, quartered

½ small cauliflower, broken into florets and blanched

2–3 new potatoes, parboiled and sliced

200 mL/7 fl oz natural yoghurt

pinch dried coriander or few fresh leaves, minced finely

grated cheese, to garnish

Place eggplant (aubergine) slices in a basin and sprinkle with sea salt; leave for 30 minutes, then drain, rinse and dry. Mix lemon juice, oil, half the mint, cumin, garlic and pepper together in a bowl, add prepared vegetables and mix gently to ensure they are evenly covered. Turn vegetables onto a lightly buttered baking tray. In separate bowl, combine yoghurt, coriander and remaining mint and set aside. Place vegetables under pre-heated hot grill and cook quickly to brown, turning as necessary for 4–8 minutes. Serve hot, accompanied by cold yoghurt and mint dressing.

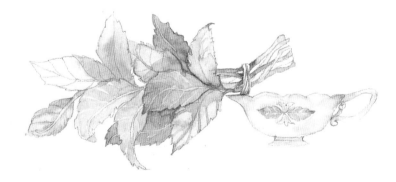

80

Mint Julep

Crush 6–8 sprigs of spearmint with 1 tablespoon each of caster sugar and water until dissolved. Add 2 jiggers of Bourbon whiskey and pour mixture over crushed ice. Garnish lavishly with mint and serve. (This is one serving. As you probably won't feel like moving after you've drunk it, make up a jug so that others can help themselves!)

TO MAKE SYRUP OF MINT — Take a quart of the Syrup of Quinces before they are full ripe, juice of mint two quarts, an ounce of Red Roses, steep them twenty-four hours in the juices, then boil it till it is half wasted, strain out the remainder and make it into a syrup with double refined sugar.

From *The Receipt Book of John Nott,* Cook to the Duke of Bolton (1723)

Mint Butter

For each 200 g/7 oz unsalted butter, prepare 4 tablespoonfuls of finely chopped mint. Soften the butter and gradually mash through mint and 1 teaspoonful lemon juice. Put butter on greaseproof paper and re-shape into a roll or ball, or press firmly into decorative moulds. Place in refrigerator to firm before serving as a garnish for grilled steak or lamb chops.

Peppermint Tea

One of Grandma's favourite remedies, this brew is very comforting to an upset stomach and will also help clear the head. It is equally refreshing served hot or icy cold, garnished with lemon twists and lots of extra mint sprigs. Use 1 teaspoonful dried peppermint leaves per cup. Put leaves in china teapot, pour over boiling water and allow to infuse for 2–3 minutes. Strain and add a little clear honey or a squeeze of lemon, if desired.

Mint 'n' Lemon Vinegar

This adds a fresh, zesty tang to salad dressings and is very simple to make. In summer, when they are at their best, pick leaves of mint and lemon-scented geranium. Wash and dry them perfectly (this is important, for if they are not properly dried the vinegar will cloud). Depending on the type and size of the bottle to be filled, you can use the leaves either whole or chopped. Put several teaspoons of both mint and geranium leaves into each bottle, then fill with white or red vinegar. Seal bottles securely and label. Another option is to retain a few perfectly formed geranium leaves, and shave some long, thin strips of lemon peel before capping jars. If you twist the peel around the leaf as you put it into the bottle, it will spiral around the geranium leaf and look most attractive. Also, using peppermint leaves will give a pleasant pinkish tinge to white vinegar.

Spearmint Bath Sachets

Mix together equal quantities of finely ground oatmeal and dried spearmint leaves. Make sachets from fabric squares, cut out with pinking shears to prevent fraying, tie with ribbon and hang from the bath tap to allow water to sluice through. The oatmeal will make the bath water feel soft and silky and the mint will add its invigorating and refreshing scent. To soothe aching joints or sore strained muscles, add 1 tablespoonful of juniper berries to each sachet and use, warm and damp, to massage affected area.

- Add mint sprigs to summer cups or cocktails for a cooling effect (mint was, in fact, once deliberately added to milk to prevent it from curdling on hot days).

- Mint enhances the first flush of spring vegetables — add the leaves to baby carrots, sugar snap peas and tiny new potatoes.

- Apple mint and pineapple mint impart a delicious flavour to summer salads and puddings or chilled desserts.

- All the mints are highly digestive, particularly peppermint, and will ease upset stomachs and hiccups. Peppermint tea induces a mild perspiration, so it is good for colds and flu.

- Old herbalists recommended rubbing bee and wasp stings with mint leaves. The 16th century herbalist Culpeper advised using a poultice of rose petals and mint leaves to cure insomnia and "help to comfort and strengthen the nerves and sinewes".

- Mints were an important ingredient in many early homemade toothpowders and pastes; peppermint water was used for cosmetic purposes and to prevent giddiness and nausea, much as smelling salts were.

Pasta and Herbs

Pasta is one of the most versatile of foods: straight or curled, thick or thin, hot or cold — it seems to be everyone's favourite. Several herb sauces go well with pasta. Pesto sauce, made from basil, Parmesan cheese, pine nuts and olive oil, is one of the best. Or, try a blend of thickened (double) cream, garlic and thyme. Stir the sauce into the freshly cooked pasta just before serving and sprinkle with grated Parmesan cheese.

Pasta and Poppy Seeds

This savoury, creamy recipe may be eaten on its own or served as an accompaniment to roast meat or goulash. It serves 6 as an entrée and 4 as a main meal.

250 g/9 oz flat egg noodles
75 g/2½ oz butter
150 g/5 oz smoked ham, diced

125 g/4½ oz breadcrumbs
2 tbsp poppy seeds

Cook noodles in boiling, lightly salted water until tender; drain. Stir in half the butter. Fry ham in remaining butter till crisp, drain on absorbent paper and then toss through pasta. Quickly fry the breadcrumbs and poppy seeds in the ham drippings until golden and crunchy. Scatter them over the dish and serve immediately.

To Make French Puffes With Greene Hearbes — Take Spinage, Parsely, Endife, a sprigge or two of Savory, mince them very fine: season them with Nutmeg, ginger and sugar. Wet them with eggs according to the quantity of the Hearbes, more or lesse. Then take the Coare of a Lemmon, cut it in round slices very thinne: put to every slice of your Lemmon one spoonfule of this stuffe. Then fry it with Sweet Lard in a Frying-panne as you frye Eggs, and serve them with Sippets or without, sprinckle them eyther with White-Wine or Sacke, or any Other Wine, saving Rennish-Wine. Serve them either at Dinner or Supper.

From *A New Book of Cookery* by John Murrel (1621)

Choko Soup

Adding small pasta shapes to this soup is a delicious and hearty variation. Marrow or squash can be used instead of choko.

*3 large chokos, peeled and
   chopped
2 onions, peeled and chopped
3 cups chicken stock*

*½ cup milk
freshly ground black pepper
cream, to garnish
snipped chives, to garnish*

Place chokos, onion and chicken stock in a saucepan, bring to boil and simmer for 20 minutes. Mash and put through sieve, or use blender. Stir in milk, and add ground pepper and dollop of cream. For the final touch, sprinkle chives on top.

Fettucine with Clams and Herbs

This recipe is perfect for alfresco dining, and it is certainly very quick to prepare, using a barbecue. The seafood provides a fresh, zesty flavour. Serves 4.

450 g/1 lb fettucine
1 onion, peeled
1½ cups small clams, cleaned
3 sticks celery
sea salt and coarsely ground
   black pepper, to taste
2 tbsp lemon juice

finely grated zest of ½ lemon
2 tbsp chopped fresh thyme
2 tbsp chopped fresh oregano
1 tbsp chopped fresh parsley
⅓ cup olive oil
½ cup pine nuts, lightly toasted
lemon wedges, as garnish

Cook fettucine according to packet instructions; drain. Coarsely chop onion, clams and celery, season with salt and pepper and mix well. Stir in lemon juice, lemon zest and fresh herbs. Heat oil in a frying pan, add clam mixture and cook quickly for 4–5 minutes. Add pine nuts and cook for a further 2–3 minutes. Toss fettucine with clam sauce and serve immediately, garnished with lemon wedges.

Honeyed Noodles with Saffron

This is derived from a Jewish recipe — adding the saffron and nuts was my idea. It is a filling and warming meal for a child, as well as a side-dish for pork or crispy fried ham.

2 eggs
2 tbsp honey
¼ tsp saffron threads
3 cups round noodles, cooked
1 tsp powdered cinnamon
pinch ground ginger
½ tsp crushed aniseed
   (optional)
¼ tsp nutmeg

1 tsp cumin
½ cup sliced cashews
½ cup sultanas
1 tbsp freshly squeezed orange
   juice
50 g/1¾ oz butter, melted
1 cup breadcrumbs
cinnamon and cream, to serve

Beat eggs and honey till fluffy. Soak saffron in a little water for 2–3 minutes then add to cooked noodles. Combine in a mixing bowl with spices, cashews, sultanas, orange juice and melted butter. Spoon into a prepared baking dish and top with breadcrumbs. Bake in a moderate oven, 190ºC/375ºF, for 30–40 minutes. Sprinkle with cinnamon and serve warm with cream poured over, or lightly whip the cream and put on the side of the dish.

Almond and Anchovy Penne

Served with salad and bread, this is ideal for 4 people as a main meal.

2 tbsp olive oil
¾ cup breadcrumbs
4 garlic cloves, peeled and
*   crushed*
450 g/1 lb penne or other
*   tubular pasta*
3–4 cups slivered almonds

3–4 anchovies, minced
1 shallot, grated
1 tsp capers
50 g/1¾ oz Feta cheese,
*   crumbled or diced*
sea salt and freshly ground
*   black pepper, to taste*

Heat oil in a frying pan and toss breadcrumbs till golden; set aside and drain on absorbent paper. Sauté garlic in remaining oil till soft; set aside. Cook penne in boiling water according to packet instructions. Drain. Toss penne with garlic, almonds, anchovies, shallot, capers, cheese and breadcrumbs in a large china bowl. Season to taste and serve immediately.

To Make Syrup Of Saffron — Take a pint of the best canary, as much balm-water, and two ounces of English Saffron; open and pill the saffron very well, and put it into the liquor to infuse, let it stand close cover'd (so as to be hot but not boil) twelve hours; then strain it out as hot as you can and add to it two pounds of double refined sugar; boil it till it is well incorporated and when it is cold, bottle it and take one spoonful in a little sack or small cordial, as occasion serves.

From *The Compleat Housewife* by E. Smith (1736)

Pesto and Noodle Soup

Accompanied by hot, crusty and extremely garlicky bread, this thick and rich soup is great for winter. Serves 4–6.

75 g/2½ oz fresh basil leaves
25 g/¾ oz grated pine nuts
1 tbsp crushed garlic
1–2 tsp sea salt
15 g/½ oz grated fresh
   Parmesan cheese
3 tbsp olive oil
a little extra olive oil, for frying
4 finely sliced leeks
4 zucchinis (courgettes), sliced
3 tomatoes, skinned and
   chopped

2–3 cauliflower florets, chopped
1 handful mixed thyme and
   parsley, chopped roughly
a few shredded cabbage leaves
1 bay leaf
2.5 L/4⅓ pts stock, preferably
   chicken
75 g/2½ oz vermicelli
50 g/1¾ oz cooked haricot
   beans

Crush basil leaves, pine nuts, garlic and salt; stir in cheese, then add the oil slowly, mixing all the while, to prepare pesto sauce base. Set aside. Heat additional oil in a skillet and gently cook leeks, zucchinis (courgettes), tomatoes, cauliflower, herbs, cabbage leaves, and bay leaf. Transfer vegetables to a large saucepan, add stock and bring to the boil. Add vermicelli and cook according to manufacturer's instructions. Add beans. Just before serving, remove from heat, lift out bay leaf and stir through reserved pesto sauce. Garnish with basil and additional Parmesan, if desired.

Spicy Walnut Sauce

This sauce may be served hot or cold with pasta, garnished with crumbled hard-boiled egg; it may also be used as a dip to accompany crudités while having pre-dinner drinks. Serves 4.

1 fresh red chilli, seeded and chopped
4 tomatoes, skinned, seeded and chopped
200 g/7 oz walnut halves, crushed
3 tbsp finely chopped fresh rosemary

2 tbsp finely chopped fresh sage
1 tsp paprika
1 tsp cayenne pepper
2 tsp sea salt
4 tbsp olive oil
2 tsp white wine vinegar

Combine chilli, tomatoes, walnuts, rosemary, sage, paprika and cayenne pepper in a bowl and mix thoroughly. Sprinkle with sea salt, cover and set aside for half an hour. Stir oil through mixture, then vinegar, then purée in blender till smooth.

Hot and Spicy

Herbs and spices add their flavours and preservative qualities to bottled pickles, chutneys and sauces. Curry spices such as cumin, coriander and turmeric are common ingredients in pickle recipes. Chillies are a favourite for flavouring fruit and vegetable chutneys. Long used by herbalists as a digestive and also to combat colds and flu, hot chillies remain a favourite today thanks to the popularity of Cajun and Eastern cuisines. Be careful when preparing chillies as they can burn the skin fiercely — avoid touching your face or eyes unless you have washed your hands thoroughly.

Pickled Mushrooms

Quick and easy to make, these pickled mushrooms keep well and make a delightful and unusual gift.

750 g/1⅔ lb mushrooms, sliced
250 g/9 oz onions, diced
2 tbsp sea salt
500 mL/17½ fl oz red wine
   vinegar
375 mL/13 fl oz red wine
¼ cup thinly sliced shallots

1 tbsp black peppercorns
4 tbsp hot red chillies, seeded
   and minced
4 blades mace
piece root ginger, peeled and
   bruised
1–2 tsp whole cloves

Place mushrooms and onions in a bowl and sprinkle with salt; cover and leave overnight. Transfer to saucepan and simmer over low heat until they re-absorb their juice. Stir in vinegar, wine, shallots, peppercorns, chillies and spices. Bring to the boil and simmer for 10–15 minutes. Let cool to room temperature and then transfer to sterilised jars. Cap securely and chill.

Spiced Elderberry Jelly

450 g/1 lb green cooking apples
   (Granny Smiths)
1.5 kg/3 lb elderberries
piece root ginger, peeled and
   bruised
1–2 tbsp sherry
1 tbsp black peppercorns

1 tsp cloves
1 cinnamon stick
1 mace blade
1 tsp allspice
water
white sugar

Chop apples roughly and place in a preserving pan with elderberries, ginger, sherry and spices. Barely cover with water and simmer until fruit is soft and pulpy. Transfer mixture to a muslin jelly bag and allow to strain overnight. Measure liquid and add 350 g/12 oz sugar for every 600 mL/1 pt fluid. Return to the saucepan and bring to the boil until mixture starts to gel. Spoon into sterilised jars and cap securely.

To Pickle Marigold Flowers — Strip the flower-leaves off, when you have gather'd the flowers, at noon, or in the Heat of the Day, and boil some salt and water; and when that is cold, put your marygold flower-leaves in a gallypot and pour the salt and water upon them; then shut them up till you use them, and they will be of a fine colour and much fitter for Porridge than those that are dry'd.

From *The Country Housewife and Lady's Director* (1732)

Spicy Tomato Chutney

A favourite of Grandma's, this chutney goes well with all meat dishes. Also serve it with a soft white cheese, such as ricotta, and plain cracker biscuits.

250 g/9 oz tomatoes, seeded, peeled and coarsely chopped
250 g/9 oz zucchinis (courgettes), sliced
250 g/9 oz onions, chopped
2 jalapeño chillies, minced
100 g/3½ oz sultanas
1 tbsp ginger, peeled and grated
1–2 tbsp olive oil

6 small dried red chillies, minced
¼ cup sliced garlic cloves
½ tsp dry mustard
½ tsp cumin
¼ tsp fenugreek seeds
200 mL/7 fl oz malt vinegar
1 tsp ground cinnamon
sea salt and sugar, to taste

Combine tomatoes, zucchinis (courgettes), onions, jalapeño chillies, sultanas and grated ginger in a bowl and mix well. Heat oil and stir-fry dried chillies and garlic with mustard and spices in a large non-aluminium preserving pan. Add tomato mixture and malt vinegar and cook slowly for about half an hour. Add sea salt and/or sugar to taste and continue to cook until consistency is thick, not runny. Allow to cool slightly and spoon into sterile jars; cap securely.

Piccalilli

Everyone's favourite pickle, Piccalilli is one of those timeless recipes that makes regular appearances at most church fetes and raffles. Try experimenting with the seasonings to make your own type of Piccalilli — fresher, saltier, spicier . . .

250 g/9 oz pickling onions
2 carrots
2 cucumbers
50 g/1¾ oz shallots
200 g/7 oz small French beans
250 g/9 oz green cherry
    tomatoes
200 g/7 oz cauliflower
2 small green chillies, peeled
    and seeded

1 tbsp sea salt
30 g/1 oz turmeric
30 g/1 oz dry mustard powder
750 mL/1¼ pt malt vinegar
4 tbsp maple syrup
1 tsp allspice
2 tbsp capers, minced (optional)

Prepare vegetables — peel onions, carrots, cucumbers and shallots; string the beans; remove stalks from tomatoes and leaves from cauliflower; and chop all into very small pieces. Mince chillies finely. Place all vegetables in an enamel or earthenware bowl, sprinkle with salt and leave for 24 hours.

Mix turmeric and mustard powder with vinegar over low heat and stir in maple syrup and allspice. Bring to the boil and pour over vegetables, then let cool to room temperature. Stir capers through, if desired. Spoon into sterilised glass jars and cap securely.

Raspberry and Redcurrant Chutney

1 orange, peeled, seeded and
   chopped
zest of 1 lemon
1 tsp finely chopped shallots
water
3 tbsp redcurrant jelly
1 cup honey
750 g/1¾ lb raspberries
12 dried prunes, seeded
   and minced

½ cup sultanas
4 figs, finely chopped
1–2 tbsp port
1 tsp French mustard
3 tbsp peeled and minced fresh
   ginger
pinch each cinnamon and
   ground ginger

Blanch orange, lemon zest and shallots in boiling water then drain well. Melt redcurrant jelly and honey together over slow heat and then add fruit, port, peel, lemon zest, shallots, mustard and spices. Simmer until liquid is slightly reduced. Spoon into sterile jars and cap securely.

Chilli Lime Pickle

This spicy, timeless pickle is a wonderful way to use up any surplus chillies and limes that you may have.

5 limes
1 tbsp whole black peppercorns
1 tbsp cumin
3 red chillies, minced
2 garlic cloves, peeled and
   crushed

1 tbsp mustard seed
1 bay leaf
300 mL/½ pt olive oil

Cut limes into small chunks and combine with peppercorns, cumin and chillies in an enamel or stainless steel bowl. Add remaining ingredients, except for oil, and fill sterilised jar(s) with the mixture. Pour sufficient olive oil into each jar to cover the spices. Make temporary lids of absorbent paper, securing them with an elastic band around the neck of each jar. Leave on a sunny windowsill for a week, and then seal firmly and store. After two or three weeks, the lime rinds will have softened and absorbed the flavour of the aromatic oil and spicy chilli. Use as a garnish for fish or chicken, or add to salads with mint sprigs or a dish of natural yoghurt as an accompaniment.

To Make Mustard — The best way of making Mustard is this : Take of the best Mustard-Seed (which is black) for example a quart. Dry it gently in an oven, and beat it to a subtle powder, and searce it. Then mingle well strong Wine-vinegar with it, so much that it is to be pretty Liquid, for it will dry with keeping. Put to this a little Pepper beaten small (white is the best) at discretion, and put a good spoonful of sugar to it (which is not to make it taste sweet, but rather quick, and to help the fermentation), lay a good Onion in the bottom, quarters if you will, and a Race of Ginger, scraped and bruised; and stir it often with a Horseradish root cleansed, which let lie always in the pot, till it have lost its vertue, then take a new one.

From *The Closet of Sir Kenelm Digby Opened* (1669)

Rosemary and Walnut Horseradish

Serve this with German-style sausages and hot meat. It is also terrific with pickled fish, like herrings.

150 g/5¼ oz grated horseradish
50 g/1¾ oz crabapples, peeled,
  seeded and grated
50 g/1¾ oz walnut halves,
  skinned and finely chopped

5 tbsp finely chopped fresh
  rosemary
1 tsp paprika
2 tbsp white wine vinegar
1 tsp sea salt
125 mL/4⅓ fl oz cream

Mix all ingredients thoroughly in a china bowl, only including cream if for immediate use. Allow to stand at room temperature before serving, so flavours may mingle thoroughly.

DILL AND COLLYFLOWER PICKLE — Boil the collyflowers till they fall in Pieces; then with some of the Stalk and most of the Flower, boil it in a part of the liquor till pretty strong. Then being taken off, strain it; and when settled, clear it from the Bottom. Then with Dill, gross pepper, a pretty quantity of Salt, when cold add as much vinegar as will make it sharp and pour all upon the Collyflower.

From *Acetaria* by John Evelyn (1699)

Tomato and Cinnamon Relish

As well as serving this as an accompaniment to cold meat as Grandma would have, try it as a dip served with crusty homemade bread.

300 g/10½ oz onions, chopped
200 mL/7 fl oz malt vinegar
juice of 1 lemon
750 g/1¾ lb tomatoes, peeled,
*   seeded and chopped*
1 tsp pickling mustard

½ tsp dry mustard
10 cm/4 in cinnamon stick
½ tsp cumin seeds
200 g/7 oz brown sugar
salt, to taste

Cook onions with vinegar and lemon juice over low heat till soft. Add tomatoes, mustard, cinnamon stick and cumin and bring to the boil. Add sugar and continue to cook until mixture thickens. Remove cinnamon stick, add salt, if desired, and spoon into sterile jars; cap securely.

A good meal sharpens the wit and softens the heart

Pickled Cabbage

Adding a bruised garlic clove and a twist of orange peel to this pickle will make it a particularly delicious accompaniment to beef.

2 firm red cabbages
75 g/2½ oz sea salt
2 L/3½ pt malt vinegar
30 g/1 oz each black
  peppercorns, allspice berries,
  cloves and mustard seed

4 blades mace
50 g/1¾ oz brown sugar
150 g/5¼ oz grated horseradish

Remove outer leaves and stalks from cabbages and shred finely. Place cabbage in a large earthenware crock or china bowl, mix well with salt and leave overnight. Spoon cabbage into wide-mouthed sterile jars. Bring vinegar to the boil and add spices, sugar and horseradish. Cook for 10 minutes and allow to cool slightly. Pour pickled vinegar over cabbage and cap jars securely.

Olive and Anchovy Marinade

Fish and meat taste superb after having been steeped in this simple marinade.

1 tbsp olive oil
2 tsp minced garlic
½ cup stoned black olives
6 anchovy fillets
2 tbsp capers, whole
1 cup sesame oil
1 cup olive oil

¼ cup vinegar
juice of 1 lemon
2 tbsp Dijon mustard
pinch ground bay leaf
1 tsp thyme
black pepper, freshly ground

Heat the tablespoon olive oil and stir-fry garlic, olives, anchovy fillets and capers briefly; (1–2 minutes); remove from heat. Whisk together sesame oil, olive oil, vinegar, lemon juice, mustard and herbs and spices, then stir through olive and anchovy mixture. Pour into sterilised jars, cap securely and refrigerate if not using immediately.

Mustard with Beer

For a more pungent mustard, increase the quantity of black mustard seeds, as these are hotter and more flavoursome than the white mustard seeds.

30 g/1 oz black mustard seeds
30 g/1 oz white mustard seeds
¼ tsp pepper
¼ tsp sea salt
pinch turmeric

¼ tsp each dried orange and
    lemon peel, grated
1 tbsp honey
1 tbsp malt vinegar
2–3 tbsp beer

Pound seeds, pepper, salt, turmeric and peel together in a mortar and pestle. Add honey, vinegar and beer, and mix to a thick consistency. Pot up in ceramic or glass jars and cap securely.

There are many simple, but efficacious remedies all around us if we country people would only develop and utilise our home resources more. In the first place, we ought to pay more attention to the raising of herbs, especially those with medicinal properties. I think we would do wisely to return to the good old custom of our grandmothers in setting aside a special bed in the garden for the cultivation of herbs.

From *The Dawn* by Louisa Lawson, "Household Hints" (c. 1888–1895)

Gingered Figs

Spiced figs, an ancient sweetmeat, are mentioned in the Bible. Delicious warm or cold, these Gingered Figs can be served with cream cheese, whipped cream or custard.

3 kg/6¾ lb figs
2 kg/4½ lb sugar
2 cups maple syrup
juice of 1 orange
1.5 L/2½ pt water
1 tbsp cloves

1 tsp cinnamon
450 g/1 lb preserved ginger,
  minced
200 mL/7 fl oz apple cider
  vinegar

Cut ends off figs and wash thoroughly. Scald figs with boiling water and allow to drain. Bring sugar, maple syrup, orange juice, water and spices and minced ginger to the boil, add figs, and cook for 3 hours. Add vinegar and cook for a further hour, or until figs appear clear. Drain and chill before serving or pour mixture directly into sterile jars and cap securely. Refrigerate till required.

Oils, Vinegars and Dressings

Herb, fruit and flower vinegars or oils are an excellent way to add flavour to dishes, while allowing you to enjoy the taste of fresh produce when the plants themselves are not readily available. Flavoured oils, vinegars and dressings add zest to salads, marinades, casseroles, grilled or sautéed dishes and even drinks. Try adding a spoonful of mulberry and pansy vinegar to frosty-cold mineral water and garnish lavishly with mint for a refreshing summer spritzer.

Oils to be flavoured should not have too strong a taste. Look for the purest, most extra-virgin olive oil you can afford, or good quality sunflower or safflower oils. Culinary herbs like thyme, rosemary, fennel, tarragon and basil tend to lose their fresh flavour and piquant fragrance when dried, but are well preserved in oil. To prepare a simple herbed oil, lightly bruise aromatic herbs and pack loosely into a glass preserving jar before covering with oil. Cap jar securely and set on a sunny windowsill — not too hot, though, or the herbs will "cook". After a fortnight, the rich plant essences should have been drawn off into the surrounding oil; taste it, and if it is not strong enough for your taste, change the herbs for fresh ones and repeat the process.

The same herbs may be used to make delicious vinegars or you might experiment with fragrant roses, violets, lavender, honeysuckle or clove pinks. It's a pretty touch to leave the flowers in the vinegar or oil to use later, rather than straining them off. Pickled rosebuds, for instance, are a delicious accompaniment to cold meats, cold savoury pies — like Melton Mowbray — or cheese. Flower vinegars usually have a lighter scent and flavour than herb or fruit ones — use them to dress fruit dishes or creamy desserts rather than meat or hot savouries. Berry or flower vinegar is delicious with fresh strawberries, or splashed onto slices of honeydew or rockmelon.

Nasturtium buds and leaves and marigold petals can also be used for oils and vinegars as Grandma well knew. Experiment with different blends of herbs, seeds and spices, varying the flavours by adding extra lemon or garlic.

Lemon thyme, basil, tarragon, marjoram flowers and salad burnet all add subtle and interesting flavours to mayonnaise or salad dressings.

Dill vinegar — so pretty with its whole seed heads floating in the bottle — is particularly delicious with fish or cold chicken dishes.

Combinations of purple basil and bruised garlic, fennel and shredded horseradish and salad burnet with savory and chopped shallots all work well, too.

Invest in the very best wine, cider, or malt vinegar available. Some moderately priced wine vinegars may lack the flavour of good aged or balsamic vinegars but are quite adequate for home preserving. Be wary of cheap commercial vinegars, however, as they may just be water added to acetic acid, and they will do nothing for the subtle flavours of the herbs or spices you wish to preserve. Check the label — some good quality vinegars indicate for how long they have been aged. If this is not shown, assume the product is the result of quick modern processing.

A tip to remember when bottling vinegar — never use metal caps as the vinegar will react with them and turn them black.

It takes four men to dress a salad: a wise man for the salt, a madman for the pepper, a miser for the vinegar and a spendthrift for the oil

Lemon Vinegar

6 lemons, sliced thinly
1 tbsp finely shredded lemon
    zest
sea salt
2 L/3½ pt cider vinegar
3 tsp white sugar

4 tbsp lemon thyme
3 tbsp lemon balm
1 tsp white mustard seeds
2 tsp grated horseradish
1 mace blade

Place lemon slices and zest in a large china bowl, sprinkle liberally with sea salt and mix well. Combine vinegar with sugar, lightly bruised herbs and spices in an enamel or ceramic saucepan, bring to the boil and simmer for 5 minutes. Pour herbed vinegar over lemon mixture, cover with a muslin cloth and leave for 4–5 days. Strain, pressing down well on lemons, pour into sterile bottles and cork securely.

Fragrant Four Herbs Vinegar

1 handful each fresh marjoram,
    oregano and savory
2 handfuls fresh thyme

5 whole cloves
500 mL/17½ fl oz white wine
    vinegar

Pick herbs for vinegar in the morning before the sun falls on them. Lightly crush all herb leaves before putting them in a glass bottle or ceramic crock with cloves. Heat vinegar in an enamel or ceramic saucepan and simmer for a few minutes. Pour over the herbs. Allow to cool slightly and then cap or cork securely. Allow to stand for at least a fortnight before use or before re-bottling as a gift.

ELDER VINEGAR — Put dryed Elder flowers into Stone or double Glass Bottles, fill them up with good wine vinegar, and set them up in the sun or by the Fire till their Virtue is extracted.

From *The Receipt Book of John Nott*, Cook to the Duke of Bolton (1723)

Basil and Mustard Vinaigrette

1 tbsp finely chopped fresh basil
5 tbsp olive oil
1 tbsp basil vinegar
1 tbsp Dijon mustard

freshly ground black pepper
pinch sugar
sea salt

Place all ingredients in a tightly lidded jar and shake thoroughly. This will transform a plain salad of tomatoes and Spanish onion rings — add chunks of seeded orange for a delicious variation.

Raspberry Vinegar

Sprinkle this on fruit salads or use in a marinade for pork ribs, or as a light sauce for chicken. It will also bring life to a vinaigrette, and poured over a tumblerful of crushed ice is a fragrant and delicious summer drink. Fruit vinegars, particularly raspberry and strawberry, were once used to soothe sore throats as well as for cosmetic purposes.

1 kg/2¼ lb fresh raspberries,
washed and picked over

1 L/1¾ pt white wine vinegar
⅓ cup caster sugar

Crush berries lightly in a large preserving jar or bottle. Combine vinegar and sugar in a ceramic or enamel saucepan, bring to the boil and simmer for 5 minutes. Pour over berries, seal jar tightly and store in a cool dark place for 2 weeks. Strain and store in sterile bottles.

Orange Vinaigrette

A refreshing accompaniment to grapefruit, pears and, of course, oranges.

juice of three large oranges
6 tbsp olive oil
3 tbsp apple cider vinegar
1 tsp finely minced onion

1 tbsp Grand Marnier
1 tbsp chopped fresh marjoram
1 tsp chopped fresh lemon or
orange thyme

Mix together orange juice, olive oil, cider vinegar, onion and liqueur and herbs in a tightly lidded jar and shake vigorously. Pour over prepared fruit and sprinkle with reserved pinch of marjoram.

Minted Balsamic Vinegar

This is an aromatic alternative to the traditional mint sauce which is usually served with the Sunday roast lamb.

2 tbsp finely chopped
peppermint
1 tbsp eau de cologne mint
1 tbsp apple mint
1 tbsp spearmint

zest of 1 orange, finely grated
1 tsp caster sugar
500 mL/17½ fl oz balsamic
vinegar

Lightly bruise all mint leaves and pack into a glass or china preserving jar along with orange zest. Sprinkle with caster sugar and then pour vinegar over, ensuring all mint is covered. Cork tightly and leave for 2 weeks before re-bottling, if desired.

Palest Pink Chive Blossom Vinegar

750 mL/1¼ pt malt or white
   wine vinegar

2 cups chive blossoms

Pack blossoms lightly into a glass preserving jar, pour vinegar over and cap securely. Place on a sunny windowsill where gentle warmth will extract the rosy colour and pungent, oniony flavour.

Baby Blue Borage and Burnet Vinegar

This has a delicate and unusual pale blue colour and a surprisingly cool, cucumber-like flavour. It's a must with salads or melon dishes.

750 mL/1¼ pt white wine
   vinegar

1 cup borage flowers
1 cup salad burnet

Prepare as for Palest Pink Chive Blossom Vinegar.

Spiced Elderberry Vinegar

1 kg/2¼ lb elderberries
1.5 L/2½ pt red wine vinegar
soft brown sugar
4–6 whole cloves

1 tsp dill seeds
½ tsp black peppercorns
½ tsp allspice berries

Lightly crush elderberries in a china bowl, traditional stone crock or preserving jar. Pour vinegar over and cover with muslin; set aside in a warm dark place for 10 days, stirring occasionally. Strain liquid and measure into an enamel or ceramic saucepan, adding 250 g/9 oz sugar to each 500 mL/17½ fl oz vinegar. Add spices and bring to the boil. Simmer for about 5 minutes, removing any scum. Strain for a second time, pour into heated sterile bottles and cap securely.

Walnut and Horseradish Marinade

2 garlic cloves, chopped and
    crushed
2 tbsp grated horseradish (note:
    only from young — not old —
    roots)
3 tbsp skinned and chopped
    walnuts

1 tbsp lemon juice
1 tsp dry mustard
freshly ground black pepper
2 cups sunflower oil

Place garlic, horseradish, walnuts, lemon juice, mustard and pepper in a bowl and mix thoroughly. Warm oil slightly and pour over. Set aside and allow to cool. The flavours will be better allowed to permeate the oil if bottled and stored, but this marinade can also be used the same day.

Middle Eastern Marinade

75 mL/2½ fl oz olive oil
150 mL/¼ pint cider vinegar
1 tsp peppermint
½ tsp cumin seed
1 tsp fenugreek
1 tbsp chopped fennel

2 chopped garlic cloves, crushed
¼ tsp coriander
pinch ground cloves
1 mace blade
1 tsp salt

Combine all ingredients and shake vigorously in a tightly lidded jar, or liquidise in a blender. This is most suitable as a basting sauce for grilled meats or as a robust barbeque condiment.

Dilly Mayonnaise

1 egg yolk
½ tsp dry mustard powder
125 mL/4⅓ fl oz olive oil
juice of ½ lemon

6 tbsp chopped dill
3 fresh sprigs tarragon, chopped
black pepper, to taste

Beat together egg yolk and mustard powder. Drip in 2 tablespoonfuls of the oil, continuing to beat mixture; then add lemon juice, then rest of oil, very slowly, beating all the while. Blanch herbs in boiling water, plunge straight into cold water and dry thoroughly. Put them through a sieve or mince by hand before quickly whisking through mayonnaise. Add freshly ground pepper, to taste.

Peppercorn Vodka

Use this as well as, or instead of, vinegar when pickling eggs, red cabbage, onions or when preparing chutneys. Add caster sugar to produce a potent, liqueur-style sweet sauce.

1 tbsp rosemary needles
1 tbsp green peppercorns
6 anise seeds

1 tsp coriander, crushed
1 tsp lemon zest
150 mL/¼ pt vodka

Bruise rosemary and combine with spices and zest. Add to vodka, cap securely and shake well. Allow to stand for at least a week before straining for use.

Hazelnut Dressing

75 mL/2½ oz hazelnut oil
1 tbsp balsamic vinegar
2 tbsp skinned crushed
    hazelnuts

1 tsp clear honey
pinch grated nutmeg
pinch salt

Combine all ingredients in a tightly lidded jar and shake vigorously before serving. Delicious with the first vegetables of spring, such as baby carrots and sugar snap peas.

Mulberry and Pansy Vinegar

This has a delicious 'bite' and a superb purple colour. You won't be able to resist turning the amethystine bottles in the light to admire them when you've finished!

1 kg/2¼ lb mulberries, washed
*   and picked over*
2 cups blue or purple pansies,
*   stems removed*

1.25 L/2 pt white wine vinegar
soft brown sugar

Crush berries lightly in a large china bowl or preserving jar with pansy blooms. Combine vinegar and sugar in ceramic or enamel saucepan, bring to the boil and simmer for 5 minutes. Pour over berry and petal mixture, cover with a cloth and leave for a day or two. Strain and measure liquid, adding 200 g/7 oz sugar for every 500 mL/7½ fl oz. Simmer together till sugar dissolves, allow to cool slightly, then pour into warmed sterile bottles and cork securely.

Green 'n' Garlicky Oil

1 tbsp watercress
1 tbsp chervil
2 garlic cloves, chopped and
*   crushed*
2 shallots, chopped
2 tbsp parsley

6 salad burnet leaves
3 fresh sprigs tarragon
olive oil
sea salt and freshly ground
*   black pepper, to taste*

Combine all ingredients in a glass preserving jar and cover with olive oil. Cap securely and store on a sunny windowsill or by a warm stove to extract colour and flavour. You may like to add bruised fennel and a teaspoon of aniseed instead of the chervil, and mix resulting oil with white wine for a delicious fish marinade. Substitute bruised rosemary leaves for the salad burnet and you have a basting sauce for barbecued lamb kebabs. Add juniper berries and you have a pork marinade . . . the possibilities are limited only by your imagination!

4
Flowers and Fruit

The Language of Flowers

There is a language little known,
Lovers claim it as their own.
Its symbols smile upon the land,
Wrought by Nature's wondrous hand;
And in their silent beauty speak,
Of life and joy to those who seek
For Love Divine and sunny hours
In the Language of the Flowers.

Traditional

Acacia — chaste love
Almond, flowering — hope
Alyssum, sweet — worth beyond beauty
Angelica — inspiration

Apple blossom — preference
Bachelor's Buttons — single blessedness
Balm — sympathy
Balsam — impatience

Basil — hatred
Bay leaf — I change but in death
Begonia — dark thoughts
Bluebell — constancy
Borage — bluntness
Box tree — stoicism
Broom — neatness, humility
Camellia — (white) unpretending
      excellence
      — (red) loveliness
Chamomile — energy in adversity
Campanula — gratitude
Candytuft — indifference
Carnation — (red) alas, my poor heart
      — (striped) refusal
      — (yellow) disdain
Christmas rose — relieve my anxiety
Chrysanthemum — (red) I love
      — (yellow) slighted love
      — (white) truth
Cistus/Rock rose — popular favour
Clematis — mental beauty
Clover — (four-leafed) be mine
Cowslip — pensiveness, winning grace
Crocus — abuse not
Cyclamen — diffidence
Daffodil — regard
Dahlia — (single) good taste
      — (double) instability
Daisy — (garden) I share your sentiments
      — (white) innocence
      — (wild) I will think on it
Elder — zealousness
Fennel — worthy of meeting all praise
Fern — sincerity

Fig — argument
Forget-me-not — true love
Foxglove — insincerity
French marigold — jealousy
Gentian — you are unjust
Geranium — (ivy) bridal favour
      — (oak) true friendship
      — (rose) preference
      — (scarlet) comforting
Gladiolus — bonds of affection
Hawthorn — hope
Heartsease/pansy — you occupy my
      thoughts
Heliotrope — devotion
Hibiscus — delicate beauty
Holly — foresight
Hollyhock — fecundity
Honeysuckle — bonds of love
Hyacinth — (purple) sorrow
Hydrangea — heartlessness
Iris — message
Ivy — friendship, fidelity, marriage
Jasmine — (white) amiability
      — (Cape) transport of joy
      — (Carolina) separation
      — (Spanish) sensuality
Jonquil — I desire a return of affection
Juniper — succour, protection
Laburnum — forsaken, pensive
Lady's Slipper — capricious beauty
      — (purple) haughtiness
Lavender — distrust
Lemon blossom — fidelity in love
Lilac — (purple) first love
      — (white) youthful innocence

Lily — (day) coquetry
Lily of the Valley — return of happiness
Lobelia — malevolence
Lotus flower — estranged love
Love-in-a-mist — perplexity
Lupin — voraciousness
Magnolia — love of nature
Marigold — grief, despair
Marjoram — blushes
Mignonette — your qualities surpass
        your charms
Mimosa — sensitivity
Mint — virtue
Mistletoe — I surmount all difficulties
Morning glory — affectation
Mulberry tree — (black) I shall not
        survive you
Myrtle — love
Narcissus — egotism
Nasturtium — patriotism
Nettle — you are cruel
Oleander — beware

Olive — peace
Orange blossom — bridal festivities
Ox Eye — patience
Pansy — thoughts
Parsley — festivity
Pea, sweet — departure
Pelargonium — (white) gracefulness
       — (red) her smile is the soul
        of witchery
Pennyroyal — flee away
Peony — shame, bashfulness
Peppermint — warmth of feeling
Periwinkle — (blue) early friendship
Petunia — never despair
Pink — boldness
   — (single) pure love
   — (variegated) refusal
Polyanthus — (crimson) the heart's
        mystery
   — (lilac) confidence
Poppy — (red) consolation
   — (white) sleep

112

Primrose — early youth, sadness
Primula — diffidence
Quince blossom — temptation
Ranunculus — you are radiant
             with charms
Rocket — rivalry
Rose — love
    — (burgundy) unconscious beauty
    — (cabbage) ambassador of love
    — (china) beauty always new
    — (dog) pleasure and pain
    — (musk) capricious beauty
    — (white) I am worthy of you
    — (yellow) decrease of love, jealousy
Rosebud — (red) pure and lovely
      — (white) girlhood, a heart
          ignorant of love
      — (moss) a confession of love
Rosemary — remembrance
Rue — disdain
Saffron — beware of success
Sage — esteem
St John's Wort — animosity
Salvia — (blue) I think of you
Scilla — (blue) forgive and forget
    — (white) sweet innocence

Snowdrop — hope
Sorrel — affection
Stephanotis — you boast too much
Stock — foresight
Sunflower — (dwarf) adoration
       — (tall) haughtiness
Sweet basil — good wishes
Sweet sultan — felicity
Sweet William — gallantry
Tansy — I declare war against you
Thyme — activity
Tuberose — dangerous pleasures
Tulip — (red) declaration of love
    — (yellow) hopeless love
Verbena — (scarlet) sensibility
      — (white) pure and guileless
Veronica — fidelity
Violet — (blue) faithfulness
    — (sweet) modesty
    — (yellow) happiness
Wallflower — fidelity in adversity
Wax plant — susceptibility
Wistaria — I cling to thee
Witch-hazel — a spell
Yew — sorrow
Zinnia — thoughts of absent friends

Lavender Blue

"The most famous of the nose-herbs is this lavender, whose flower spike, as modest in hue as a Quaker's bonnet, is highly fragrant," wrote Louise Beebe Wilder in *The Fragrant Garden*. Lavender has as many ancient and romantic connotations as the rose. Sometimes referred to as "Our Lady's Candlestick", lavender's scent is thought, indeed, to be a heavenly one — for when the Virgin Mary spread the Infant Jesus' clothes on a lavender bush to dry, she is said to have bestowed its perfume in gratitude.

Many historical "receipts" feature lavender and its household and culinary uses have long been known. It was the Romans who originally associated lavender with freshness — the very name "lavender" is derived from the middle Latin *lavare*, meaning "to wash". Traditionally, lavender was used as a strewing herb for floors and cupboards in an attempt to keep the atmosphere sweet and clean in days when houses lacked protection from the damp. The dried flowers were placed in beds and oaken presses where they perfumed clothes and handkerchiefs, causing Izak Walton to sigh longingly in 1653: "Let's go to that house for the linen looks white and smells of lavender and I long to be in a pair of sheets that smell so". Apart from enjoying the cheerful homely scent, housekeepers knew lavender was a powerful weapon against moths, silverfish and other insects.

Lavender has several therapeutic benefits — Queen Elizabeth I, who was known to suffer from migraines, would quaff up to 10 cups a day of lavender tea to soothe her fretful brow. Royal patronage of this wholesome herb continues with lavender-scented cosmetics being a firm favourite with Queen Elizabeth II.

Lavender and Musk Cologne

Make this simple, elegant scent yourself, using freshly picked flowers from the garden.

500 mL/17½ fl oz water
2 cups lavender flowers
1 tbsp rose-scented geranium
   leaves
1 tbsp lemon verbena leaves

1 tsp grated orange rind
2 tbsp brandy
30 drops bergamot oil
2–3 drops musk oil

Pour water over flowers, leaves and orange rind; cover and steep for two days. Chill, strain and stir brandy and essential oils through mixture. Store in an atomiser and keep in the refrigerator to refresh yourself on a gaspingly hot summer's day.

LAVENDER WATER — Put two pounds of lavender pipps in two quarts of water; put them into a cold still, and make a slow fire under it; distill off very slowly into a pot till you have distilled all your water, then clean your still well out, put your lavender into it and distill it off slowly again; put it into bottles and cork well.

From *The New Art of Cookery* by Richard Briggs, many years Cook at the Globe Tavern, Fleet Street, the White Hart Tavern, Holborn, and the Temple Coffee House (1788)

Lavender and Rosemary Tea

A soothing tea, this has the added bonus of rapidly easing a headache.

6–8 lavender flowers	*boiling water*
1 tbsp rosemary flowers	*honey, to taste*
1 tsp dried lemon peel	

Combine flowers and peel in a china or glass teapot. Pour boiling water over and steep for five minutes before straining and pouring into warmed china cups. Add honey, if desired.

Lavender Wand

A favourite gift is the lavender-scented "bottle" or wand, made from stalks of lavender plaited with narrow ribbon. They were traditionally used in the linen presses of large country homes to separate sheets, towels and pillowslips into dozens and half-dozens.

To make a lavender wand, take about 30 freshly picked lavender flowers on stalks as long as possible. Tie stalks below flowers with narrow mauve ribbon about 1 m/1 yd long. Bend the stalks back gently below the ribbon so they form a cage over the flowers. Weave the long ends of the ribbon in and out of the stalks, moving down until the flower heads are covered. Stitch ribbon ends securely and finish with a bow.

CONSERVE OF THE FLOWERS OF LAVENDER — Take the flowers being new so many as you please, and beat them with three times their weight of White Sugar, after the same manner as Rosemary flowers, they will keep one year.

From *The Queen's Closet Opened* by W.M., Cook to Queen Henrietta Maria (1655)

Lavender and Mustard Seed Chutney

A spicy pickle which goes well with all cold meats, especially lamb.

3 lemons
sea salt and coarsely ground
*   black pepper, to taste*
apple cider vinegar
1 cup lavender flowers, finely
*   chopped*

2 tbsp mustard seed
3 onions, diced
60 g/2 oz sultanas
cinnamon stick
allspice and sugar, to taste

Chop lemons into small pieces and remove pips. Place in a mixing bowl and sprinkle well with salt and pepper. Cover with vinegar and let stand for 24 hours. Place lemons in a saucepan and add remaining ingredients. Bring to the boil, then cover and simmer till lemon is well softened and liquid reduced. Remove cinnamon stick. Spoon chutney into sterile glass jars and cap securely.

Lavender and Ginger Jelly

This is a pleasant accompaniment to roast pork, duck or rabbit.

2 cups lavender flowers
125 g/4½ oz jellied ginger root,
*   chopped*
boiling water

juice of 2 lemons
sugar
30 g/1 oz liquid pectin
2 tsp ground ginger

Place flowers and chopped ginger in a bowl and barely cover with boiling water. Cover and allow to steep for 24 hours. Strain pulp through a muslin jelly bag and add lemon juice. Measure liquid and for every cup of lavender-ginger infusion, add 2 of sugar. Bring mixture to the boil and boil hard for 1–2 minutes. Add liquid pectin and continue to boil, being careful not to let it boil over. Remove pan from heat and carefully remove any scum from the surface. Stir in ground ginger and continue to stir for 2–3 minutes. Let stand for 10–15 minutes. A few fresh lavender flowers can be stirred into the jelly, if desired. Pour into sterile glass jars and cap securely.

A SWEET-SCENTED BATH — Take of Roses, Citron Peel, Sweet Flowers, Orange Flowers, Jessamy, Bays, Rosemary, Lavender, Mint, Pennyroyal, of each a sufficient quantity, boil them together gently and make a Bath to which add Oyl of Spike six drops, musk five grains, Ambergris five grains.

From *The Receipt Book of John Middleton* (1734)

Lavender Toffee

An old-fashioned favourite at children's parties and church fetes.

1 cup lavender flowers, bruised
450 g/1 lb caster sugar
100 mL/3½ fl oz water

pinch cream of tartar
1 tbsp apple cider vinegar

Grease a shallow tin (20 x 30 cm/8 x 12 in) with butter. Place lavender flowers in a small muslin bag and tie loosely. Place sugar, water, cream of tartar, lavender bag and vinegar in a non-alumunium saucepan and bring to the boil. Boil rapidly for 10 minutes or until mixture clarifies (i.e., it should look like clear honey). Remove from heat, take out lavender bag and pour toffee into tin. As mixture cools, mark surface into squares with a sharp knife.

Lavender and Apricot Tart

700 g/1½ lb canned apricot
*   halves, drained*
½ cup lavender flowers, finely
*   minced*
1 cup dried apricots, finely
*   chopped*
2 eggs

½ cup caster sugar
3 tbsp ground almonds
2 tbsp sour cream
3 tbsp icing sugar
4–6 sheets frozen short crust
*   pastry*

Drain tinned apricots and combine in a bowl with minced lavender and dried apricots. In a separate bowl, beat eggs and sugar till mixture thickens. Add almonds and sour cream and mix well. Line a pie dish (25–30 cm/10–12 in diameter) with pastry and spoon apricots and lavender evenly over it. Spread almond mixture evenly over this. Bake in a hot oven, 240ºC/475ºF, for 10 minutes, then reduce heat to 180ºC/350ºF and bake for 20–25 minutes or until done. Dust with icing sugar and decorate with crystallised lavender flowers.

Lavender Wash Balls

Elizabeth I is said to have bathed with soap balls made from powdered or grated herbs, which would have been more like pumice stones than the soap we use today. However, if herbs and flowers are pulverised thoroughly in a mortar and pestle, they will not have an abrasive effect.

> 150 g/5 oz Castile soap, grated
> 125 mL/4⅓ fl oz rosewater
> lavender essential oil
> 1 tsp dried and finely crushed
>   marjoram
> 2 tbsp dried and finely crushed
>   lavender flowers
>
> 1 tbsp dried and finely crushed
>   rose petals
> mauve vegetable colouring
>   (optional)

Melt soap and combine with rosewater over a low flame, stirring all the while with a wooden spoon. Cool slightly and knead to make a paste. Add oil, marjoram and flowers, and colouring, if desired. Roll mixture into balls and leave in the sun on a piece of greaseproof paper for about two hours. Wet your hands with a little extra rosewater and lavender oil and "polish" each ball till smooth. Leave to dry completely overnight.

119

~• This is a delightful French custom, derived from the medieval use of "casting bottles" of perfume: fill an atomiser with lavender water and use when steaming out stubborn wrinkles. A quick method of making lavender water is to add 3–4 drops of essential lavender oil to 150 mL/5 fl oz of warm water.

~• Remember how Grandma's wooden furniture used to gleam so? By adding lavender oil to your dusting rag, you can have a similar sheen on precious woodwork.

~• Decorate an immaculate white linen table napkin, on which a terrine or pâté is displayed, with two or three lavender flowers.

~• Crumble a handful of lavender flowers over soft white cheese (cream cheese or ricotta) before serving with crackers.

Sweet Bloomin' Violets

The tiny violet is one of the world's most cherished flowers. In the language of flowers, sweet violets mean modesty, blue signal faithfulness and yellow happiness. There were said to be violets growing in the shade of olive groves in ancient Athens and the Greeks used the flowers as a motif for their city. Known as Aphrodite's favourite flower, a posy of violets bears a message of love. Napoleon was probably the most famous devotee of violets. Josephine wore violets on her wedding day and, every year thereafter Napoleon sent her violets to mark their anniversary. Before leaving for his final exile in Saint Helena, he asked to visit Josephine's grave where he plucked violets. After his death, these were discovered in a locket around his neck.

Violets are edible as well as sweetly ornamental. Did you know the leaves make a delicious addition to a mixed green salad? A wine made from the flowers was very popular in Roman times, and violet vinegar, made by steeping the flowers in white wine vinegar, has a beautiful colour and fragrance. The delicate taste lends itself well to soft creamy desserts, such as the traditional French *vyolete,* a pudding made from mashed violets, milk, honey and flour. Crystallised or sugared violets are easy to prepare and add an enchanting touch to cakes or little fancy sweetmeats. Violet leaves make an attractive base for holding jellies or moulds and the flowers may be used as a garnish for chilled fruit soups with a dollop of sour cream or natural yoghurt.

121

These whimsical flowers were mentioned often by Homer and Virgil and were used by herbalists "to moderate anger" and "to comfort and strengthen the heart". Pliny prescribed a liniment of violet roots and vinegar for gout and spleen disorders and he also advised that a chaplet of violets worn around the head would "dispel the fumes of wine" and prevent headaches. A compress of violet, strawberry leaves and poppy seeds was thought helpful for countering sleeplessness. Violets may be used to make soothing skin tonics and fresheners, too.

Fragrant Violet Hair Rinse

1 cup violet flowers   *1 tbsp lavender flowers*
1 cup rose petals   *500 mL/17½ fl oz boiling water*

Place flowers in boiling water and infuse for 15–20 minutes. Remove from heat and leave to steep a further 30 minutes. Strain and store in the refrigerator. After shampooing hair, pour the scented water through, without rinsing out, to leave hair sweet-smelling and clean.

Violet Eye Bath

All parts of the violet are considered to have medicinal value. Early herbalists used the flowers for cleansing wounds and soothing respiratory tract infections. This gentle wash will ease and refresh strained or reddened eyes.

1 tbsp violet flowers, very   *150 mL/¼ pt distilled water*
*   carefully rinsed*   *25 mL/1 fl oz rosewater*
1 tbsp rose petals

Combine flowers, distilled water and rosewater in a small non-aluminium saucepan over gentle heat for 5–10 minutes. Allow to cool then strain off violets and discard. Bottle in a clean sterile jar, cap securely and store in refrigerator. Use to bathe eyes or to make soothing, cooling eye compresses.

Violet Leaves, at the entrance of Spring fried brownish and eaten with Orange or Lemon Juice and Sugar is one of the most agreeable of all the herbaceous dishes.

From *Acetaria* by John Evelyn (1699)

Violet Lemonade

1 cup violets
juice of 6 lemons
750 mL/1¼ pt mineral water

sugar, to taste
crushed ice and fresh violet
flowers, to garnish

Place violets in a china bowl, mix with lemon juice and refrigerate overnight until juice turns pink. Strain off violets and add juice to pitcher of chilled sparkling mineral water. Add sugar (or more lemon juice), to taste, stir through crushed ice and float a few violets on top before serving.

Violet Syrup

Modern-day herbalists use violet syrup as both a gargle and a laxative. Heated, it is thought to have soothing effect on asthma and coughs.

2 cups violets　　　　　　　　*300 g/10½ oz sugar*
400 mL/14 fl oz boiling water　　*squeeze lemon juice, to taste*

Bruise flowers and place in a china bowl. Pour water over, cover and infuse for 30 minutes. Strain off liquid through muslin, pressing down well on flowers. Reheat liquid gently, stirring in sugar with a wooden spoon until it has dissolved. Bring mixture to the boil and simmer till syrupy. Add lemon juice, to taste. Remove from heat and allow to cool slightly before pouring into a clean sterile bottle and capping securely.

A MOST PRECIOUS OINTMENT FOR ALL MANNER OF ACHES AND BRUISES; AND ALSO FOR THE REDNESS OF THE FACE — Take Violet, Primrose, Elder, Cowslip, leafs and flowers; Sage, Mugwort, Ragweed, White Lillies, St Johnswort, Smallage, Marjoram, Lavender, Sothernwood, Rosemary, Rose-leafs, Rue, Fetherfew, Tansie, Lovage, Mint, Camomile, Thyme, Dill, Clary, Oak of Jerusalem, Penyroyal, Hysop, Balm, White Mint, Marygold, Peony-leafs, Bay-leafs, Saffron, each one handful. Stamp all these in a Stone-mortar, as you get them then put them into a Pottle of Sallet Oyl, and so let them infuse there till you have all the rest together; for you cannot get them all at one time, but get them as fast as you can. Then put to them and the Oyl a quart of White Wine, and set it over the fire, and boyl it to the Consumption of the Wine; then take if off and strain it; then put it into a glass and keep it for use. When you annoint any sore with this do it by the fire side, chafing it well in; and then lay a Hog's bladder next to it, and a Linnen upon that.

From *Receipts in Physick and Chirurgery* by Sir Kenelm Digby (1668)

Violet Honey

450 g/1 lb clear honey   *1 cup violets*

Place honey in a double saucepan over low heat and add violets; cook gently for 30 minutes. Remove from heat, cover and store in a warm place for a week or so, giving mixture an occasional stir. Gently reheat honey, strain off violets, pour into clean sterilised jars and cap securely.

Violet and Apple Wine Cup

6 tbsp violets   *1 bottle dry white wine*
long thin strip of apple peel   *90 mL/3 fl oz Calvados brandy*
sprigs of lemon thyme

Place violets, apple peel, lemon thyme and wine in a bowl and mix gently. Cover and keep in a cool place for 24 hours. Strain off scented wine and pour into pitcher or punch bowl. Stir through Calvados, chill slightly and serve in glasses garnished with crystallised violets.

Violet Cleansing Milk

An ancient Gaelic recommendation exhorted young lasses to ". . . rub . . . [their] faces with violets and goats' milk and there is not a prince in the world who will not follow thee". This cleansing milk is very gentle and especially useful for those with sensitive or troubled skin — though I don't guarantee any princes!

1 cup violet flowers   *400 mL/14 fl oz whole milk*

Place flowers in a small non-aluminium saucepan with the milk and bring to the boil, stirring constantly. Remove from heat and allow to infuse for 1–1½ hours. Strain milk well, bottle in a sterile container and refrigerate. To apply, dip moistened cottonwool balls into the violet milk and smooth gently over face and neck before rinsing off with tepid water and patting dry with a soft towel.

Violet Facial Steam

½ cup violet flowers
½ cup orange blossoms
1 tbsp lime flowers

1 tbsp chamomile flowers
boiling water

Place flowers in a large china bowl and half fill with boiling water. Tenting head with a towel, lean over fragrant vapour and steam-cleanse face for 10–15 minutes. After cleansing, wipe face gently with moistened tissue or cloth and close pores with a skin freshener.

Plums with Violet Custard

450 g/1 lb plums, halved and
    stoned
4 tbsp rosé wine
75 g/2½ oz demerara sugar
1 vanilla pod

175 mL/6 fl oz milk
150 mL/¹/₄ pt thickened (double) cream
1 cup violet flowers
3 egg yolks
crystallised violets, to garnish

Preheat oven to 200⁰C/400⁰F. Arrange plums in a deep, ovenproof baking dish (10 cm/4 in diameter) with wine, 50 g/1¾ oz of the sugar and the vanilla pod. Cover and bake for 20 minutes then allow to cool completely. Remove vanilla pod. Combine milk, cream and violet flowers in a double saucepan over low heat. Simmer for 5–10 minutes but do not allow to boil; remove from heat and strain off violets, pressing gently against non-metallic sieve. Beat egg yolks and slowly beat in about 3 tablespoons of the heated violet milk mixture, then stir all back into saucepan. Continue to stir over low heat till custard thickens, then cover and allow to cool slightly. Pour custard over cooled plums and sprinkle with rest of sugar. Cook quickly under hot grill until sugar caramelises then garnish with crystallised violets and serve immediately.

Roses, Roses, Roses

If you already have roses in your garden, your nose will tell you which are the most likely to provide fragrance, but if you're wondering which roses to buy and grow, a few suggestions might be helpful. Among the most fragrant roses are the older, cottage-style varieties. These include the Damask *(Rosa damascena),* Cabbage *(R. centifolia)* and *Rugosa* roses. Use roses to prepare soothing, scented cosmetics, delicate jams, syrups and ices as well as romantic potpourris and sachet mixes.

Rose Scented Linen

Add 250 mL/9 fl oz rosewater to the final rinse when washing delicates such as silk or broderie anglaise. Sprinkling rosewater over sheets before ironing them will fill them with sweet fragrance.

Rosewater Hand Softener

This old recipe is wonderful for roughened and chapped hands.

3 tsp cornflour	*juice of 1 lemon*
125 mL/4⅓ fl oz rosewater	*2 tbsp glycerine*

Blend cornflour with rosewater and heat gently. Add lemon juice and glycerine and simmer, stirring until mixture thickens slightly. Pour into a clean, sterile jar, cool and cap securely. Stored in the refrigerator this recipe will keep for up to one month.

TO MAKE OYNTMENT OF ROSES — Take oyle of Roses four ounces, white wax one ounce, melt them together over seething water then chafe them together with Rose-water and a little white vinegar.

From *The Treasurie of Hidden Secrets and Commodious Conceits* by John Partridge (1586)

Rose Petal Bavarois

This is a refreshing and fragrant summertime dessert.

1 cup pink rose petals, lightly bruised	*1 tbsp gelatine*
	3 tbsp water
200 mL/7 fl oz milk	*400 mL/14 fl oz thickened*
4 egg yolks	*cream*
100 g/3½ oz caster sugar	

Remove white "heel" from rosebuds and infuse rose petals in milk over low heat for 15 minutes. Remove from heat and process petals with milk in blender. Return flavoured milk

128

to heat and bring just to boil. Whisk together egg yolks and sugar in a double boiler until sticky. Gradually pour in flavoured milk and stir constantly over low heat until mixture becomes thick and creamy. Pour into a bowl and allow to cool slightly. Dissolve gelatine in water and blend into rose custard; continue to cool mixture until it is just about to set. Whip cream into soft peaks and fold gently through custard. Spoon into a decorative mould or individual ramekins and chill to set. Serve with frosted rose petals.

Romantic Rose Potpourri

125 g/4½ oz red rose petals
75 g/2½ oz jasmine flowers
30 g/1 oz orange flowers
12 bay leaves, crushed
4 tbsp lavender
30 g/1 oz sandalwood chips
4 tbsp cardamom seeds,
   crushed

2 tbsp cinnamon
1 tbsp crushed cloves
1 tbsp crushed orange peel
3–4 tbsp orris root powder
12 drops rose oil
5 drops musk oil

Dry all flowers and leaves until they are crisp. Using your hands, mix them together with spices and orris root powder in a large earthenware or glazed terracotta crock. Add oils, one drop at a time and finally the citrus peel. Display potpourri in a pretty floral china dish or on an antique silver tray.

TO CANDY ROSE LEAVES AS NATURAL AS IF THEY GROW ON TREES — Take of your fairest Rose leaves, Red or Damask, and on a sunshine day sprinkle them with Rose-water, lay them on one by one on a fair paper, then take some double refined sugar beaten very fine, put it in a fine lawne searse when you have laid abroad all the Rose leaves in the hottest of the Sun, searse sugar thinly all over them and anon the Sun will candie the sugar; then turn the leaves and searse sugar on the other side, and turn them often in the sun, sometimes sprinkling Rose-water and sometimes searsing Sugar on them, until they be enough, and come to your liking, and, being thus done, you may keep them.

From *The Whole Body of Cookery Dissected* by William Rabisha (1675)

Spiced Rose Beads

Exchanging scented jewellery was once very fashionable. Try making a pretty piece for yourself or a friend. The fragrance intensifies with the warmth of the skin and will last many years.

400 g/14 oz red rose petals   *4 tbsp orris root powder*
water   *4 tbsp gum tragacanth*
1 tsp ground cinnamon   *rose oil*
1 tsp ground cloves   *hat pin and fishing line*

Place rose petals in a non-aluminium saucepan and just cover with water. Simmer — do not allow to boil — for 1 hour, then cover and put aside for 24 hours. Repeat this process three times; you should then have a smooth, mushy paste. Blend cinnamon, cloves and orris root powder in a separate bowl, add gum and blend this to a paste. Combine mixtures and blend thoroughly. Dip your hands into rose oil, pick up pinches of the mixture and roll in your palms to form beads. Place on greaseproof paper and leave overnight. Take hat pin and, dipping in oil, pierce each bead and string it on the line. Wrap in tissue and store in a warm, dark, airy place for six weeks, or till quite hard.

Pickled Rosebuds

*1 cup baby pink or crimson
rosebuds, tightly furled
200 mL/7 fl oz white wine or
apple cider vinegar*

*1 tbsp clear honey (clover or
apple blossom, preferably)
few sprigs woodruff*

Remove white bitter "heel" from rosebuds and pack firmly into a wide-mouthed sterile glass jar. Combine wine or vinegar with woodruff and honey over a low heat then pour into jar, ensuring no air bubbles are left between flower buds. Cap securely and store jar in a warm sunny place for a fortnight, shaking regularly. The pickled rosebuds are a delicious accompaniment to cold meats, cheese or game dishes and pink-tinged rose-flavoured vinegar left over is refreshing with salads.

❧ Make rose ice cubes by putting one bud and a curling twist of lemon rind in each compartment of an ice tray, then cover with slightly diluted rosewater. Float ice cubes in a glass pitcher of chilled rosé wine, or strawberry fruit punch.

❧ Weave a wreath of deep crimson roses and place it about the rim of a bowl containing a sinfully dark and delicious chocolate mousse.

❧ For a special little girl's birthday cake, fill the layer between two plain cakes with rose petal jelly. Make icing by combining equal parts of icing sugar and softened butter with finely minced pink rose petals and spread over top and sides of cake. Roll cake in shredded coconut and decorate top with perfect pink rose petals.

Berried Treasure

Strawberries, those crimson jewels of the woodland, are the most delicious of fruits. There is evidence that strawberries have been enjoyed since antiquity — strawberry seeds have been excavated from Roman forts and the "straberie" was listed in the Household Roll of the Countess of Leicester in the eleventh century. These were most likely wild strawberries (*Fragaria vesca*) and picked by village women and children. When it was discovered these berries could command good prices, they were strung through their tops on pieces of straw to ensure successful transportation to market — hence one derivation of their name.

The wild strawberries were long held in esteem in Europe because of their exquisite flavour, although the berries' tiny size — less than 1 centimetre (½ in) — made harvesting and preparation tedious. Wild strawberries were planted on a grand scale by King Charles V of France (1364–80) — he ordered 1200 plants to be grown in the Royal Gardens of the Louvre in Paris. It was this wild strawberry species which was cultivated and gardeners progressively improved on size and even colour, giving us most of the modern varieties we enjoy today. However, it is still the tiny-fruiting wild strawberries which produce the most delicate flavour.

Fresh strawberries make marvellous cosmetics and are particularly useful as a dentifrice. Because of their acid content, eating fresh strawberries will help reduce discolouration of tooth enamel.

Wonderful complexion fruit, strawberries help brighten and soften a sallow or dry skin. A cut strawberry rubbed over the face will whiten skin and reduce inflammation. Strawberry juice may also be blended with soybean oil and cocoa butter to produce a refreshing cleanser, especially suitable for oily skin.

An excellent source of vitamins A and C, strawberries have been used in treating rheumatism and gout. The leaves have astringent properties and may be taken whole or as an infusion to treat gastro-intestinal upsets. And, of course, fresh strawberries can be eaten in a great variety of ways including fruit salads, by themselves with different toppings, in a refreshing sorbet served between courses, and in mousses, pies, jams and sauces. Although some say strawberries are perfect without embellishment, you may like to try them dipped in natural yoghurt with a pinch of allspice . . . or with a squeeze of lemon juice or freshly ground black pepper . . . or in one of the other ways suggested here.

Strawberry and Marshmallow Cream

This is an excellent moisturiser, and is most useful for dry or mature skin as the marshmallow has a softening effect.

150 mL/¼ pt distilled water
2 tbsp marshmallow root
    powder
1 tbsp clear honey
30 g/1 oz lanolin

10 g/⅓ oz beeswax
1 tsp rosewater
4–6 strawberries, mashed
8 drops benzoin tincture

Add water to marshmallow root powder, stir and simmer. Strain and add honey. Melt lanolin and beeswax together in a double saucepan over low flame and stir through liquid, slowly adding rosewater and strawberry pulp. Beat till thick and fluffy. Add benzoin and beat again till mixture cools thoroughly, otherwise it will separate. Pot up for future use in a sterile lidded jar and keep in refrigerator.

Strawberry Summer Pudding

This is a traditional British recipe, redolent of warm afternoons watching the cricket. Sprinkle with cinnamon and serve with custard or cream.

*1 loaf white bread, thinly sliced
   with crusts removed
250 g/9 oz strawberries,
   washed and hulled
400 g/14 oz mixed soft fruits
   (equal quantities of
   redcurrants, blackberries and
   raspberries are the traditional
   combination)*

*2–3 tbsp white sugar
grated zest of 1 orange
75 mL/2½ fl oz apple juice*

Lightly butter a china pudding bowl and line with slices of bread, overlapping and cutting them to fit evenly. Place berries in a non-aluminium saucepan with sugar, orange zest and apple juice. Cover and bring to the boil; simmer gently for 1 minute or until fruit softens slightly. Reserve 3 tablespoonfuls juice before spooning fruit into bread-lined bowl, pressing down well. Cover top with slices of bread, trimming and tucking in edges to fit. Put a china plate on top and secure with a heavy weight (e.g. cans). Refrigerate overnight. To serve, carefully run a blunt-edged knife between basin and bread. Turn pudding out onto plate and drizzle reserved juice over it, as desired.

POTTAGE WITHOUT THE SIGHT OF HERBS — Mince several sorts of sweet herbes very fine — Spinage, Parsley, Marigold Flowers, Succory, Strawberry and Violet Leaves. Pound them with oatmeal in a mortar. Boil your oatmeal and herbs in broth and serve.

From *The Receipt Book of John Nott,* Cook to the Duke of Bolton (1723)

Strawberry Ambrosia

In this recipe the flavour and scent of the fruit is enhanced by the honey and rosewater.

1 small honeydew melon
1 punnet strawberries, washed
* and hulled*
250 g/9 oz seedless green
* grapes*

1 cup coconut, freshly grated
2 cups rosé wine
2 tbsp honey
½ cup rosewater

Remove seeds from melon and scoop out flesh with a melon-baller. Combine in a bowl with strawberries and grapes and coconut. Stir wine, honey and rosewater together in a separate bowl or jug and pour over fruit. Chill for several hours before serving as a starter.

Stimulating Strawberry Tea

This blend is a terrific blood purifier. Take several times a week for any complexion problems, such as acne.

2 tsp strawberry leaves, dried
1 tsp raspberry leaves, dried

1 tsp woodruff, dried
250 mL/9 fl oz water

Bring water to the boil and add leaves; simmer for 5–10 minutes. Strain and sweeten, if desired. *Note*: a stronger tincture may be made by simmering a handful of the dried leaves in equal parts of water and almond oil to cover, until liquid is reduced by a third. Sieve the oil-leaf mixture and pot up for later use as a first aid treatment for cuts and burns.

Strawberry Cordial

This is easy to make and has endless uses — dilute it with iced water for a summer drink, with hot milk during winter, or use neat as a delicious sauce for puddings.

4 punnets strawberries, cleaned and hulled	1 tbsp jellied ginger root
15 g/½ oz nutmeg	1 tsp coriander
15 g/½ oz cloves, powdered	1 cinnamon stick
	150 g/5¼ oz clear honey

Purée strawberries in blender and place in a saucepan. Add all other ingredients and simmer over low heat until mixture becomes syrupy; cool. Remove cinnamon stick before pouring into sterile lidded bottle. Refrigerate until use.

STRAWBERRY AND ALMOND TANSY — Take four quarts of new milk and half a pound of the sweet almond flour, two ounces of lemon juice and half a pint of strawberry juice. Put to these two pounds of fine sugar and a quart of Canary. Stir them together and beat them till they froth and become of a pleasant colour.

From *The Good Housewife's Handmaid* (1585)

Strawberry and Madeira Sauce

I love this with fruit or a creamy dessert, but it is also a good accompaniment to poached fish.

2 punnets strawberries, washed, hulled and halved	madeira wine
1½ cups caster sugar	sour cream

Place strawberries and sugar in a glass or china storage jar and cover with madeira wine. Seal jar and store for 2 weeks in a cool, dry place. When sauce is required, put berry mixture in food processor with a dollop of sour cream and blend till smooth.

Strawberry and Buttermilk Soup

A simple, fresh-flavoured soup, this is a delicious starter for a summer evening.

*2 punnets strawberries, washed
    and hulled
2 cups water
½ cup buttermilk
½ cup orange juice*

*juice of 1 lemon
1 tbsp chopped fresh woodruff
¼ cup raw sugar (optional)
200 g/7 oz natural yoghurt
mint sprigs, to garnish*

Bring berries, water, buttermilk, orange juice, lemon juice, chopped woodruff and sugar to the boil in a non-aluminium saucepan; simmer gently for 10 minutes. Cool slightly, purée in blender, then chill thoroughly. Stir 1 tablespoon of yoghurt through each portion and garnish with mint before serving immediately.

Strawberries with Tarragon Cream

The tarragon adds an unusual but delightful taste and aroma to this salad.

*1 mignonette or iceberg lettuce
2 punnets strawberries, washed
    and hulled
1 tbsp chopped walnuts
watercress, to garnish*

*Dressing
juice of ½ lemon
1 tsp brown sugar
4 tbsp thickened (double) cream
1 tsp fresh tarragon*

Arrange washed and dried lettuce leaves on a serving plate with strawberries and walnuts on top; set aside. In a separate bowl, whisk together lemon juice and sugar. Lightly whip cream, then fold in lemon mixture. Add tarragon. Spoon dressing over top of strawberry-walnut mixture, garnish with watercress if desired and serve immediately.

A large Pottle of ripe strawberries, picked and put into a bason with two spoonfuls of Sugar, a pinch of powdered cinnamon, a gill of Brandy. Currants and raspberries the same. Stir gently and serve.

From *Shilling Cookery for the People* by Alexis Soyer (1855)

Honey-Currant Glazed Strawberries

These are delicious served with coffee, or accompanied with lashings of cream as a light dessert.

150 g/5¼ oz unsweetened redcurrant jelly
1–2 tbsp honey
1 strip orange rind

1 tsp cinnamon
pinch allspice
2 punnets strawberries, washed, with stems retained

Combine jelly, honey, rind, cinnamon and allspice over a low heat in a double saucepan. (*Tip*: a small metal whisk will produce a smoother glaze than a spoon.) Holding each berry by its stem, dip into warm glaze mixture, then place on greaseproof paper, glazed side up. Chill for half an hour to harden.

Strawberry and Pecan Jam

2½ cups strawberries, washed and hulled
2 cups rhubarb, rinsed and diced
1 cup seedless raisins
1 cup diced pineapple

3 cups sugar
½ cup orange peel
½ cup finely chopped pecan nuts
⅓ cup liquid fruit pectin

Combine strawberries, rhubarb, raisins, pineapple, sugar and orange peel in a large, non-aluminium saucepan. Cover and set aside for at least 12 hours. Bring slowly to the boil and cook for 5 minutes, stirring constantly to stop mixture sticking to pan. Add pecans and pectin and remove from heat, still stirring and skimming off any scum that arises. Continue stirring for 5–10 minutes, or until mixture approaches gel stage, to keep fruit and nuts in suspension. Spoon into clean, sterile jars and cap securely.

Strawberry and Pansy Salad with Hazelnut Dressing

1 mignonette or iceberg lettuce
1 punnet strawberries, washed
    and hulled
1 mango, peeled and sliced
10 snow peas, blanched
1 cupful pansy blooms, gently
    rinsed and patted dry

Dressing
1 tbsp hazelnut oil
2 tbsp lemon juice
1 tbsp ground hazelnuts
black pepper, freshly ground

Tear lettuce into bite-sized pieces and place in bowl with strawberries, mango pieces, snow peas and pansy blooms. Combine dressing ingredients in lidded jar and shake vigorously before tossing through salad — *very* gently so as not to bruise the flowers. Serve immediately.

Sweet 'n' Sour Strawberries

*2 punnets strawberries, washed
and hulled
juice of 1 lemon
juice of 1 orange
cinnamon stick*

*3 tbsp soft brown sugar
200 mL/7 fl oz sour cream
1 tbsp pistachio nuts
pinch nutmeg*

Place strawberries in a non-aluminium saucepan with juices, cinnamon and 2 tbsp sugar; simmer for 1–2 minutes and remove from heat. Remove cinnamon stick and place berries and liquid in serving dish. Spread sour cream over berries. Combine extra sugar, pistachios and nutmeg and sprinkle over cream. Place briefly under hot grill to caramelise sugar and serve immediately.

- To make strawberry wine, chill white or rosé wine in a jug and garnish with slices of orange, strawberries and fresh sweet woodruff.

- Add strawberries to melon balls, fruit punches and salads; float sliced berries in sparkling mineral water garnished with mint and white strawberry flowers.

- Mouth ulcers may be reduced by boiling strawberry hulls and rinsing the cooled, strained water through the mouth. This also reduces tartar on the teeth.

- Arrange strawberries, with their stems attached, around two bowls. Fill one with whipped cream and soft brown sugar and the other with orange juice and the zest of a lemon. Use strawberries to dip alternately into different mixtures.

- Sun-dried strawberries are a tangy garnish for salads and desserts. They are also a tasty snack and can be used in cheese platters. To prepare, hull the berries, place on a fine mesh drying rack and cover with muslin. Leave in the sun for 3 consecutive days, bringing them in at night-time to avoid the dew. Store in airtight glass jars till ready for use.

Bibliography

Beebe Wilder, L. *The Fragrant Garden*. Dove Publications, New York, 1974.

Berkley, R. *Berries: A Cookbook*. Cassell, London, 1990/Simon & Schuster Australia, Sydney, 1990.

The Country Women's Association of Western Australia. *The CWA Cookery Book and Household Hints*. E. S. Wigg & Son Pty Ltd, Perth, 1936.

Creber, A. *Oils and Vinegars*. Angus & Robertson, Sydney, 1990.

Crumpacker, E. *Seasonal Gifts*. William Morrow & Co., New York, 1983.

Duff G. *A Book of Potpourri*. Orbis Publishing London, 1985.

Duff, G. *A Book of Herbs and Spices*. Merehurst, London, 1987.

Duff, G. *Natural Fragrances*. Doubleday, Sydney, 1989.

Dutton, N. *Presents From Your Garden*. Nelson, Australia, Melbourne, 1986.

Forsell, M. *Herbs*. Anaya Publishers, London, 1990.

Fulton, M. *Preserves and Pickles*. Octopus, London, 1984.

Garland, S. *The Herb and Spice Book*. Weidenfeld & Nicholson, London, 1979/ Doubleday, Sydney, 1984.

Goode, J. and Wilson, C. *Fruit and Vegetables of the World*. Lothian, Melbourne, 1987.

Grieve, Mrs M. *A Modern Herbal*. Penguin, London, 1980.

Grigson, J. *Jane Grigson's Fruit Book*. Penguin, Ringwood, 1982.

Guyton, A. *A Woman's Guide to Natural Beauty*. Thorsons, London, 1981.

Hayes, A. B. *Beauty From the Garden*. Sally Milner Publishing, Sydney, 1991.

Hayes, A. B. *Country Scents*. Night Owl Publishers, Shepparton, 1989.

Hayes, A. B. *Healing From the Garden*. Sally Milner Publishing, Sydney, 1991.

Hemphill, J. and R. *Herbs and Spices*. Omega, London, 1984/Paul Hamlyn, Sydney, 1974.

Hemphill, J. and R. *Herbs: Their Cultivation and Usage*. Blandford, London, 1984.

Hemphill, R. *Herbs for All Seasons*. Penguin, Ringwood, 1972.

Horrocks, L. *Natural Beauty*. Angus & Robertson, London/Sydney, 1980.

Klienmann, K. and Slavin, S. *On Flowers*. William Collins Australia, Sydney, 1988.

The Language of Flowers. Michael Joseph Ltd, London, 1968.

Lee, V. *Traditional Gifts*. Conran Octopus, London, 1990.

Leyel, Mrs C. F. *Herbal Delights*. Faber & Faber, London, 1937.

Mackenzie, T. *The Giving Garden*. William Collins Australia, Sydney, 1987.

Milo Orbach, B. *The Scented Room*. Doubleday, Sydney, 1987.

Orr, S. *The Gourmet's Garden*. Ure Smith, Sydney, 1975.

Pescott, Mrs L. *Early Settler's Household Lore*. Raphael Arts Pty Ltd, Richmond, 1977.

Purchon, N. and Clary, D. J. *Herbcraft*. Hodder & Stoughton, Sydney, 1990.

The Q & A Collection. ABC Books/William Collins Pty Ltd, Sydney 1983.

Rose, J. *Kitchen Cosmetics*. Panjandrum Books, California, 1986.

Sandell, C. (ed.) *The Book of Cures*. Collins, Sydney, 1988.

Sanecki, K. N. *The Book of Herbs*. Doubleday, Sydney, 1985.

Sinclair Rohde, E. *A Garden of Herbs*. Dover Publications, New York, 1969.

Spencer, E. *Cakes and Ale*. Stanley Paul & Co., London, 1897.

Stockwell, C. *Nature's Pharmacy*. Arrow, London, 1988.

Stone, J. *The Alcoholic Cookbook*. Michael Joseph, London, 1972.

Thomas, A. *The New Vegetarian Epicure*. Penguin, London, 1978.

Tolley, E. and Mead, C. *Herbs*. Sidgwick & Jackson Ltd, London, 1986.

Tomnay, S. *Herbs*. Leisure Magazines, Sydney, 1988.

Treben, M. *Health From God's Garden*. Thorsons, London, 1987.

Trueman, J. *The Romantic Story of Scent*. Aldus/Jupiter, London, 1975.

Walden, H. *Flower Works*. Windward, Leicester, 1987/Simon & Schuster, Australia, Sydney, 1987.

Wickham, L. *Grandma's Favourite Remedies*. Bay Books, Sydney, 1988.

Wilson, G. *The Time is Ripe*. Viking O'Neill, Melbourne, 1988.

Index

143